Talk Portuguese

Cristina Mendes-Llewellyn

Series editor
Alwena Lamping

BBC Languages

Published by BBC Worldwide Ltd
Woodlands, 80 Wood Lane, London W12 0TT
First published 1998
Reprinted and updated 2004

© BBC Worldwide Ltd 2004
ISBN 0563 51903 7

Printed and bound by Martins the Printers Ltd, Berwick-upon-Tweed

Developed by BBC Languages
Edited by Sarah Boas
Additional editing by Eric Smith and Melanie Kramers
Project Manager Alexis Chung
Project Editor Tamsen Harward
Design management by Book Creation Services
Design by Avril Broadley for BCS
Illustrations by Sylvie Rabbe for BCS
Typeset by Gene Ferber for BCS
Cover design by Carroll Associates
Cover photographs: Michelle Chaplow (tl, tr, b); Pictor (back)
Audio producer: John Green, tefl tapes
Sound Engineer: Tim Woolf
Presenters: Stefa Boje; João Ferreira; Ana-Cristina Pisarro;
    Victoria Willing
Studio: Robert Nichols Audio Productions and Q Sound
Music by: Peter Hutchings

Contents

Introduction   4
Pronunciation guide   6

1 Bom dia!   7
saying hello and goodbye
introducing yourself
getting to know people

2 Donde é?   15
talking about your nationality
saying where you're from
saying what you do for a living
giving your phone number
using the numbers 0 to 10

3 Este é o Paulo   23
introducing someone
talking about your family
saying how old you are
talking about another person
using the numbers 11 to 100

4 Um café, por favor   31
ordering a drink in a bar
offering, accepting or refusing
paying for your drinks
using the numbers 100 to 30,000

Ponto de controle 1   39
progress check 1

5 Desculpe, onde é a estação?   43
asking where something is
asking for help with the answer
talking about where you live and work

6 Há um banco aqui perto?   51
finding out what there is in town
. . . and when it's open
making simple enquiries
understanding directions

7 Quanto custa?   59
asking and understanding the price
describing and commenting
buying food in a shop or market

Ponto de controle 2   67
progress check 2

8 Queria um quarto   71
checking in at a hotel
finding a hotel room
booking ahead by phone
making requests

9 A que horas parte?   79
asking if there is a bus or coach
checking train times
buying tickets
checking travel details

10 Bom apetite!   87
reading the menu
asking about items on the menu
ordering a meal
saying what you like and don't like
paying compliments

Ponto de controle 3   97
progress check 3

Reference Section
Audio scripts and answers   101
Grammar   119
Portuguese – English Glossary   123

Introduction

Welcome to **Talk Portuguese**, the BBC's new Portuguese course for absolute beginners. Designed for adults, learning at home or in a class, it provides the ideal introduction to Portuguese, covering the basic language needed in everyday situations on a visit to Portugal. It is suitable if you want to learn for work, for fun and in order to prepare for a first level qualification.

Talk Portuguese is an interactive course consisting of a book and two 60-minute CDs or cassettes of recordings made by native Portuguese speakers. Although designed to be used with the audio, the book could be used separately, as the audio scripts are included in the reference section. Free tutor's support and activities are available online at http://www.bbclanguages.com/talk/.

Talk Portuguese encourages you to make genuine progress and promotes a real sense of achievement.
The key to its effectiveness lies in its structure and its systematic approach. Key features include:

- simple step-by-step presentation of new language
- involvement and interaction at every stage of the learning process
- regular progress checks
- useful hints on study skills and language learning strategies

How to use Talk Portuguese

Each of the ten units is completed in ten easy-to-follow steps.

1   Read the first page of the unit to focus on what you are aiming to learn and to note any key vocabulary in the *Em Portugal* section. This provides useful and relevant information on Portugal and sets your learning in context.

2   Listen to the key phrases on the CD or cassette – don't be tempted to read them first. Then listen to them again, this time reading them in your book too. Finally, try reading them out loud before listening one more time.

3   Work your way, step by step, through the activities which follow the key phrases. These highlight key language elements and are carefully designed to

develop your listening skills and your understanding of Portuguese. When you hear the activity number, pause the recording and read the instructions before you listen. To check your answers, refer to the *Audio scripts and answers* starting on page 101.

4   Read the *Em português* explanations of how the language works as you come to them – they are placed just where you need that information.

5   When you have completed the activities, and before you try the *Put it all together* section, close your book and listen to the Portuguese conversations straight through. The more times you listen, the more familiar the language will become and the more comfortable you will become with it. You might also like to read the dialogues at this stage.

6   Complete the consolidation activities on the *Put it all together* page and check your answers with the *Audio scripts and answers*.

7   Use the language you've learnt – the presenters on the cassettes/ CDs will prompt you and guide you through the *Now you're talking!* page as you practise speaking Portuguese.

8   Check your progress. First, test your knowledge with the quiz. Then check whether you can do everything on the checklist – if in doubt, go back and spend some more time on the relevant section. You'll have further opportunities to test your knowledge in each *Ponto de controle* after units 4, 7 and 10.

9   Read the learning hint at the end of the unit, which provides ideas and suggestions on how to use your study time effectively or how to extend your knowledge.

10 Finally, relax and listen to the whole unit, understanding what the people are saying in Portuguese and taking part in the conversations. This time you may not need the book so you can listen to the recordings on their own.

Boa sorte! Good luck!

Pronunciation guide

The best way to acquire a good Portuguese accent is to listen to the cassettes or CDs often and to imitate the speakers closely.

1 **Vowels** which carry the stress of a word are clear and consistent, but when unstressed they often almost disappear.

	a	e	i	o	u
	falo	ela	bica	come	custa
as in . . .	hat	sell	meet	olive	root

Before **n**, **nh** or **m**, and in some vowel combinations, they are nasal – said through the nose and mouth together:

n**ão**	b**em**	v**inho**	b**om**	m**un**do

2 Most **consonants** are similar in Portuguese and English, but the following need attention:

			as in . . .
c	+ e or i; ç before a, o, u	centro, você	lace
	+ all other letters	copo	cat
ch		chamo	shop
g	+ e or i; and j	gelado, hoje	usual
	+ u and all other letters	gosto	got
h	always silent	hoje	
nh		vinho	onion
r	in middle/between vowels	tarde	very
	beginning/doubled – trilled	rua, carro	rock
	at end – soft	morar	maker
s	at beginning/after consonant	sim	sun
	between vowels	casa	maze
	end/middle before consonant	inglês	shoe
z	at beginning/middle	prazer	zebra
	at end	faz	ash

3 As a general rule, words are stressed on the last but one syllable (**obrigado**) or the final one (**café**). Accented vowels always carry the stress.

1 UM

Bom dia!

- ● **saying hello and goodbye**
- ● **introducing yourself**
- ● **getting to know people**

Em Portugal . . . (In Portugal . . .)

how you greet someone will depend on how well you know them and your relationship to them. Shop assistants, bank clerks and waiters will be formal in their greetings, even though you may have known them for years.

When meeting someone for the first time you usually shake hands. Close friends and relatives will give each other a kiss on each cheek. Men may also give each other a friendly pat on the back.

Saying hello . . .

I   Listen to these key phrases.

Bom dia	Hello, good morning
Boa tarde	Hello, good afternoon
Boa noite	Hello, good evening
Como está?	How are you?
Bem . . .	Well, fine . . .
obrigado, obrigada	thank you (m./f.)
. . . e você?	. . . and you?

You say **obrigado** if you are a man and **obrigada** if you are a woman.

2   Listen as Paula de Oliveira, a waitress at the Café Central, greets two of her customers. What greetings does she use?

> Bom dia, Senhora Paula

.............................., **Senhora Barbara.**
.............................., **Senhor António.**

Em português . . . (In Portuguese . . .)

you address a man as **Senhor** and a woman as **Senhora**. You usually add the person's name if you know it:

   Senhor António   Senhora Barbara

A woman can also be addressed as **Dona**:

   Dona Paula or **Senhora Dona Paula**

When followed by a surname, **Senhor** means Mr and **Senhora** Mrs or Miss.

3   In the evening another regular customer arrives. How does she ask Paula how she is?

What does Paula reply? Fill in the gaps.

Vanda	**Boa noite, Dona Paula.** ....?
Paula	**Bem** ...., e ....?

. . . and goodbye

4 Listen to these key phrases.

Adeus	Goodbye
Tchau	'bye
Até logo	See you later

Bom dia, **boa tarde** and **boa noite** are also used to say goodbye, or to wish someone a nice day, afternoon or goodnight.

5 Senhora Barbara, Senhor António and Vanda say goodbye as they leave. What does each one say?

Adeus, boa tarde

Senhora Barbara ....…..….....................

Senhor António ....…..….....................

Vanda ....…..….....................

6 At which of these times of day would you say the following? Match the times with the greetings.

08.00	**Boa noite, Senhor Luís.**
14.00	**Adeus, bom dia.**
23.00	**Boa tarde, Senhora Fernanda.**

7 If you were staying at a hotel in Portugal, how would you greet the following people and ask them how they are?

- at 2.00 p.m.   Senhor Pedro, the hotel porter.
- at 10.00 a.m.   Ana, the porter's teenage daughter.
- at 9.00 p.m.   Senhora Paula, the receptionist.

8 As you go out, how would you say goodbye to:

- Senhor Pedro at 5 p.m. ?   • Senhora Paula at 11 p.m. ?

Introducing yourself . . .

1 Listen to these key phrases.

(Eu) sou	I am
Você é . . . ?	Are you . . . ?
O Senhor é/A Senhora é . . . ?	Are you . . . ? (formal)

Em português . . .

when saying who you are, you normally insert the word for 'the'
before your name:

o before a male name or **Senhor**:

    Sou o Pedro   **Sou o Senhor Reis**

a before a female name or **Senhora**:

    Sou a Carla   **Sou a Senhora Costa**

When asking someone's name formally you also use **o** and **a**:

    O Senhor é o . . . ?   **A Senhora é a . . . ?**

2 At your hotel you overhear a client introducing himself to the
receptionist. What is his name?

Paulo Morais   João Morais   João Reis

3 A client whom the receptionist doesn't recognise arrives at the hotel.
How does she introduce herself?

Receptionist	**A Senhora é?**
Ana	.... **a Ana da Costa Passos.**
Receptionist	**Ah, Dona Ana. Como está?**

4 Two teenagers meet in the foyer. Notice that they greet each other
with the informal **Olá** (Hi) and **Tudo bem?** (Everything OK?).
How do they say their names?

Fernando	**Olá, ... Tu és?**
Sandra	.... **Tudo bem?**

. . . and getting to know people

5   Listen to these key phrases.

Como se chama?	What's your name?
Chamo-me . . .	My name is . . .
Muito prazer	Pleased to meet you
Desculpe?	Pardon?

6   At the café, Luís de Castro and Vanda Abreu have just met. Tick the key phrases you hear.

7   Vanda calls a friend of hers over to join them, but Luís doesn't quite catch her name. What does he say?

Carla	**Olá! Chamo-me Carla Correia.**
Luís	................................?
Carla	**Chamo-me Carla, Carla Correia.**
Luís	**Muito prazer.**

Em português . . .

there is more than one way of saying 'you'. Use:

o Senhor/a Senhora	to someone you don't know well, an older person, your boss
você	to someone of similar age and background as you, e.g. a work colleague, fellow student
tu	to a friend, family member, young person

The choice affects other words:

o Senhor	**é . . .**	**como se chama?**	**como está?**
você	**é . . .**	**como se chama?**	**como está?**
tu	**és . . .**	**como te chamas?**	**como estás?**

8   Carla's daughter is with her and Luís wants to know her name. He asks her: **Como te chamas?** What does she say?

Put it all together

1 How would you say the following in Portuguese?

a How are you?
b Pleased to meet you
c Have a nice day!
d I am
e Goodnight
f Goodbye
g What's your name?

Now complete the crossword. The answers above provide the clues.
Note that only part of each phrase is used in the crossword.

a) ⬜ ⬜ T ⬜
b) ⬜ U ⬜ ⬜ ⬜
c) D ⬜
d) ⬜ O ⬜ ⬜
e) B ⬜ ⬜
f) ⬜ ⬜ E ⬜
g) ⬜ ⬜ ⬜ M
?

2 What are they saying?

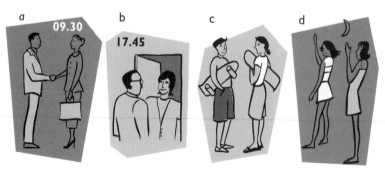

a   b   c   d

Now you're talking!

1   Imagine you are Carla Correia and you have just arrived at the hotel reception.

   ◊ **Bom dia, a Senhora é . . . ?**
   ◆ Introduce yourself.
   ◊ **Desculpe?**
   ◆ Repeat your name.
   ◊ **Ah! sim, a Senhora Dona Carla Correia!**

2   It's 9 p.m. and you are in the hotel bar. A businessman greets you and introduces himself.

   ◊ **Boa noite. Chamo-me Carlos Ribeiro.**
   ◆ Say you are pleased to meet him.

3   The following day in a shop you meet Mr Ribeiro again. He greets you.

   ◊ **Boa tarde, Dona Carla, como está?**
   ◆ Say you are well and ask him how he is.
   ◊ **Eu também estou bem, obrigado.**
   ◆ Say you'll see him later.

4   Imagine you have dropped into Paula's café. You're sitting at a table and a couple with their daughter join you. The parents introduce themselves.

   ◊ **Boa tarde. Chamo-me Paulo.**
   ◊ **Eu chamo-me Ana.**
   ◆ Introduce yourself and ask the girl her name.
   ◊ **Chamo-me Sandra.**
   ◆ Later, say goodbye to them all.

Quiz

1 How would you ask a child his or her name?
2 What does **Muito prazer** mean?
3 When do you use **Boa noite**?
4 Is Pedro a man's name or a woman's name?
5 If someone says to you **Como está?** how do you answer?
6 Which is more informal: **tu** or **você**?
7 How would you say 'See you later'?
8 Rearrange these letters to find a word meaning 'goodbye':
   DUAES

Now check whether you can . . .

■ greet someone correctly during the day – morning, afternoon and evening

■ say goodbye

■ introduce yourself

■ reply when someone is introduced to you

■ ask someone's name

■ ask someone how they are

■ reply when someone asks you how you are

■ ask for clarification if you didn't catch what was said

Listen to the audio as often as you can and try to imitate the voices as closely as possible. Listening to and repeating the phrases many times will help you get used to the sounds of Portuguese and remember them. Don't worry about making mistakes when you speak at this stage. Just keep practising!

Donde é?

- **talking about your nationality**
- **saying where you're from**
- **saying what you do for a living**
- **giving your phone number**
- **using the numbers 0 to 10**

Em Portugal . . .

you will find people are generally warm and friendly. Their relaxed manner and native courtesy make it easy for visitors to feel at home. If they like you, you may well be invited to their home for a typical Portuguese dinner, or be given a guided tour of the area. It is therefore worth learning to say a few things about yourself and showing interest in their culture. Be prepared to answer lots of questions about yourself and your country but do ask some questions too!

15

Talking about your nationality . . .

1 Listen to these key phrases.

É inglês?	Are you English?
Sim – sou inglês	Yes – I'm English
Não – não sou inglês	No – I'm not English
Sou irlandês	I'm Irish
Donde é?	Where are you from?
Sou de Londres	I'm from London
Sou de Lisboa	I'm from Lisbon

2 Three students meet for the first time in a Portuguese language school. Listen as their teacher Maria asks them their nationality and tick them as you hear them.

	italiano	irlandês	inglês
estudante 1			
estudante 2			
estudante 3			

Em português . . .

there are several different types of adjectives (words used to describe people and things, e.g. French, married, big, green). To describe someone's nationality, you will find two main types of endings:

1	**-o**	(for a man)	**italiano**	**americano**
	-a	(for a woman)	**italiana**	**americana**
2	**-ês**	(for a man)	**inglês**	**português**
	-esa	(for a woman)	**inglesa**	**portuguesa**

3 Maria says her nationality, then asks two more students where they are from. Listen and fill in their nationalities.

Maria   ....

Anna   ....

Robert   ....

. . . and saying where you're from

4   Here are some countries and nationalities. Fill in the feminine forms of
    the nationalities, then listen and check your answers with the audio.

País		Nacionalidade	
Espanha	*Spain*	espanhol	*espanhola*
País de Gales	*Wales*	galês	
Inglaterra	*England*	inglês	
Alemanha	*Germany*	alemão	*alemã*
Escócia	*Scotland*	escocês	
França	*France*	francês	
América	*America*	americano	
Brasil	*Brazil*	brasileiro	
Irlanda	*Ireland*	irlandês	

Listen out for the sound change in the consonant **s** in **inglês**,
escocês, **francês**, etc when **-a** is added for the feminine.

5   Now listen as Maria talks to three more students, Véronique (French),
    Tom (English) and Katie (Scottish). How do they give their nationality
    and say where they come from? Fill in the gaps.

Maria	**Donde é, Véronique?**
Véronique	**Sou ...., de ....**
Maria	**E você, Tom?**
Tom	**.., de ....**
Maria	**E você, Katie, é ....?**
Katie	**Não, ..., sou ...., de**
	....

6   How would you ask:

- Andrew if he is Scottish?
- Mary if she is Irish?
- Sean if he is American?
- Carla if she is Italian?

If their nationalities are correct, how would they all answer? And if
Mary is American, not Irish?

Saying what you do for a living

1 Listen to these key phrases.

O que faz?	What do you do?
Sou recepcionista	I'm a receptionist
Não sou jornalista	I'm not a journalist
A Senhora é secretária?	Are you a secretary?
Sim, sou	Yes, I am
Não, não sou	No, I'm not

2 Listen to three people talking about what they do for a living. Who is an artist (**artista**), who is a dentist (**dentista**) and who is a student (**estudante**)?

Note that 'a' or 'an' is not used when saying what you do.

Ana Fortes   Pedro Correia   Manuel de Oliveira

3 Some professions have a masculine form (ending in **-o** or **-or**) and a feminine form (ending in **-a** or **-ora.**).

Maria asks three students where they come from and what their jobs are. Can you fill in the details?

Nome	Cidade	Profissão
Madalena	....	....
Fernando	....	....
João	....	....

cantor/a singer
pintor/a painter
médico/a doctor
professor/a teacher
desempregado/a unemployed
reformado/a retired

Em português . . .

as well as meaning 'you are', **é** also means 'he/she is', 'it is'

Giving your phone number

1 Look at the following handwritten numbers and note how 1 and 7 are written. Now listen and repeat them.

0	1	2	3	4	5	6	7	8	9	10
zero	um	dois	três	quatro	cinco	seis	sete	oito	nove	dez

2 Listen to these key phrases.

Tem telefone?   Do you have a phone number?
Sim. É o 97 95 65.   Yes. It's 97 95 65.

Notice that you say **o** (the) before the number.

3 Listen to four people asking for each other's phone number and put them in the order in which you hear them. The first one has been done for you.

a   891 5467   ....   b   31 32 92   (*1*)
c   020 7582 2456   ....   d   977 3632   ....

4 Senhora Ferreira rings directory enquiries to find out two phone numbers (**números**). What are they?

Travel agency   ....…...........
Doctor's surgery   ....….............

5 Now practise saying the following phone numbers.

a   723 44 55   b   894 98 33
c   020 7562 1432   d   00 44 20 8894 7161

6 Practise saying your work and home number and those of your friends and relatives.

Put it all together

1 **Países** (countries). Can you find nine countries hidden in the word search below?

K	I	A	L	L	O	N	D	E	R	S	I
P	I	N	G	L	A	T	E	R	R	A	N
A	H	N	A	U	O	A	E	L	I	L	G
D	L	E	S	C	A	N	A	D	Á	E	L
N	A	S	L	I	B	I	Ç	A	O	M	A
A	Q	P	L	I	O	R	N	I	G	A	M
L	E	Á	D	I	S	E	A	S	D	N	A
R	T	N	R	U	X	Q	R	S	E	H	T
I	Y	H	A	S	A	J	F	O	I	A	E
L	N	A	E	S	C	Ó	C	I	A	L	R

2 Complete the following dialogue by filling each gap with a word from the box:

Anne   **Bom .... Como .... chama?**
Martin   **Chamo-me Martin. E ....?**
Anne   **................. Anne. ....
francesa. Você ....
americano?**
Martin   **Não, sou inglês. Sou .... Devon.**
Anne   **Eu sou de Paris. O que ....?**
Martin   **................. jornalista.**
Anne   **Eu sou professora.**

sou
dia
chamo-me
sou
se
de
é
faz
você

3 Match the answers to the questions:

a	**O Senhor é italiano?**	**Sou artista.**
b	**Donde é?**	**Sim, sou inglês.**
c	**A Maria é africana?**	**Não, sou português.**
d	**É inglês?**	**Sim, de Angola.**
e	**Tem telefone?**	**Sou de Moçambique.**
f	**O que faz?**	**Sim. É o 977 1221.**

Now you're talking!

1 Imagine that a Portuguese friend has arranged a meeting for you with his cousin Fernando.

 ◆ Say who you are and where you are from. Ask him where he is from.
 ◇ **Sou de Braga.**
 ◆ Ask him what he does for a living.
 ◇ **Sou pintor.**
 ◆ Ask him for his phone number.
 ◇ **Sim. É o 275 6777.**

2 Your name is Mr Perry. You have just booked a room at the Hotel do Mar. The receptionist asks you a few questions.

 ◇ **O Senhor Perry é inglês?**
 ◆ Say no. Tell her you're Welsh.
 ◇ **Donde é?**
 ◆ Tell her you're from Glamorgan.
 ◇ **O Senhor tem telefone?**
 ◆ Say your telephone number is 00 44 339 5411.

3 You have been introduced to Ana Mancini, a student who is learning Portuguese.

 ◆ Ask her if she is Italian.
 ◇ **Sim, sou. Sou de Roma.**
 ◆ Ask her if she is an artist.
 ◇ **Não, não sou. Sou professora.**

4 Here are four words you have met in this unit. Try to pronounce them and then check your pronunciation with the recording.

 ● **João**   ● **profissão**   ● **alemão**   ● **não**

Quiz

1   Rearrange these letters to find a number:
    TROQUA.
2   How would you say 'I'm not English'?
3   Complete this sentence: **Eu .... de Lisboa**.
4   How would you ask a man if he is Brazilian?
5   Someone asks you if you are American and you happen to be Irish,
    so what would you reply?
6   If someone asks you the question **O que faz?** what do they want to
    know?
7   How do you ask for someone's phone number in Portuguese?
8   Which numbers are missing in the following sequence?
    um .... três quatro .... seis.
9   How do you say 'I'm a student'?

Now check whether you can . . .

■   say what nationality you are

■   ask where someone comes from and say where you're from

■   say what your job or profession is and ask others for this
    information

■   understand and use the numbers 0 to 10

■   ask someone for their phone number and give your phone number

When you come across new words, it is a good idea to write them
down in a notebook. Remember that it is easier to remember words
when they are in a context, so try to learn a few phrases connected
with those words too.

3 TRÊS

Este é o Paulo

- **introducing someone**
- **talking about your family**
- **saying how old you are**
- **talking about another person**
- **using the numbers 11 to 100**

Em Portugal . . .

the family is perhaps the most important thing in society. A generation ago many couples would have had large families. Nowadays, however, changes in lifestyle and financial pressures have made smaller families more popular. The Portuguese love children; in cafés and restaurants they are always made welcome, even late in the evening. If you have children of your own, you'll find that even people you don't know will suddenly start chatting to your child or will offer him or her a sweet.

Introducing someone

1 Listen to these key phrases.

Este é o . . .	This is . . . (to introduce a man)
Esta é a . . .	This is . . . (to introduce a woman)

2 Listen as Paulo introduces two people to Ana Pereira at a business conference, then complete the conversations.

Paulo	**Bom dia, Senhora Pereira.**
	.... é o Senhor Luís Correia.
Luís	**Muito prazer.**
Paulo	**E .... é a Senhora Carla Fortuna.**
Carla	**Muito prazer.**

Em Portugal . . .

professional titles such as **Advogado** (lawyer), **Engenheiro** (engineer), **Doutor** (a graduate in any profession as well as a medical doctor) are often used. **O Senhor Doutor Engenheiro** and **O Senhor Doutor Advogado** are also commonly used when introducing people.

3 Now listen to Paulo introducing some more people and make a note of their professions.

Nome	Doutor/a	Engenheiro/a	Advogado/a
Francisca Martins			
Roberto Leal			
Mário de Andrade			
Luisa Teixeira			

4 How would you introduce the following to someone else?

- António Leal
- Dona Sofia Pereira
- Senhor Carlos Fortuna
- Engenheiro Fernando Correia

Talking about your family

1 Listen to these key phrases.

É casado?/É casada?	Are you married?
Sou casado/a, solteiro/a	I'm married, single
Tem filhos?	Do you have any children?
Sim. Tenho um filho	Yes. I have a son
. . . e uma filha	. . . and a daughter
Não, não tenho filhos	No, I don't have any children

'One' or 'a' is **um** before a male, **uma** before a female.

2 Doutor Ferreira asks Doutora de Sousa about her family. How does she say she has a son and a daughter? Tick the key phrases you hear.

Does Doutor Ferreira have any children?

Em português . . .

there are different words for 'my'.

o meu before a male		**a minha** before a female	
esposo	husband	**esposa**	wife
pai	father	**mãe**	mother
irmão	brother	**irmã**	sister

3 Doutora de Sousa introduces some of her family. How does she say who Marta, Pedro and José are?

Esta é .... irmã Marta, este é .... irmão Pedro e este é .... pai José.

4 In the student canteen, Fernando asks Carla if she has any **irmãos** (brothers or sisters). He asks the question with the familiar form **tens**. What is Carla's reply?

(eu) tenho I have
(tu) tens you have (informal)
(você) tem you have (formal)

Saying how old you are

1 Listen to some of the following numbers between 11 and 100.

11 **onze**	21 **vinte e um**	40 **quarenta**
12 **doze**	22 **vinte e dois**	50 **cinquenta**
13 **treze**	23 **vinte e três**	60 **sessenta**
14 **catorze**	24 **vinte e quatro**	70 **setenta**
15 **quinze**	25 **vinte e cinco**	80 **oitenta**
16 **dezasseis**	26 **vinte e seis**	90 **noventa**
17 **dezassete**	27 **vinte e sete**	100 **cem**
18 **dezoito**	28 **vinte e oito**	
19 **dezanove**	29 **vinte e nove**	
20 **vinte**	30 **trinta**	

31 to 99 follow the same pattern as 21 to 29

2 You will hear all but one of the following numbers. Which one is missing?

37   **92**   **57**   **69**   **78**

3 Listen to these key phrases.

Quantos anos tem? (você)	How old are you?
Quantos anos tens? (tu)	How old are you?
Tenho dezanove anos	I'm 19
Tenho vinte e dois anos	I'm 22

4 Sofia meets Cristina and Miguel at a disco and asks them how old they are. Tick the key phrases you hear. How old are they?

5 Doutora de Sousa wants to find out the age of one of her students. How does she ask Fernando how old he is? How does he give his age?

Doutora de Sousa   **Quantos anos ....?**
Fernando   ....

Talking about another person

I Doutora de Sousa finds out more about Fernando and his family.
Listen, then say if each of these statements is **verdadeiro** (true)
or **falso** (false):

		V	F
a	Fernando's son is called Miguel.		
b	His daughter is called Teresa.		
c	His son is five.		
d	His daughter is six.		

2 Listen to Maria, Alexandra and Daniel introducing their families and
decide which family belongs to whom.

a ....   b ....   c ....

Put it all together

1   Paula de Oliveira is introducing her family. Can you fill in the family tree?

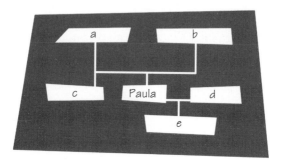

O meu esposo chama-se **Pedro.**
A minha filha chama-se **Ana.**
A minha mãe chama-se **Luisa.**
O meu pai chama-se **Manuel.**
O meu irmão chama-se **Carlos.**

2   Paula de Oliveira plays bingo every Wednesday. Below is her card and a list of numbers. Look at the list and cross out the numbers on her card.

cinquenta e nove   **cinquenta e cinco**   **vinte e três**
treze   **quinze**   **trinta e um**   **trinta e nove**

13		15	16		20
22	23		25		27
31		33			39
50		55			59

3   If someone ask you **Tem filhos?** or **Tem irmãos?** would you say **Sim** or **Não**? If **Sim**, can you give details?

Now you're talking!

1   Imagine that you are Luís Correia at Paula's café and she asks you about your family.

◇ **É casado?**
◆ Say yes, you are married.
◇ **Tem filhos?**
◆ Tell her you have a son, and his name is David.
◇ **Quantos anos tem?**
◆ Say he is 26.
◇ **É casado?**
◆ Say yes, he is married.
◇ **Tem filhos?**
◆ Tell her he has no children. Now ask if she is married.
◇ **Sim, sou casada.**
◆ Ask if she has any children.
◇ **Eu tenho uma filha. Ela chama-se Ana.**
◆ Ask her how old she is.
◇ **Tem quinze anos.**

2   Ana, who works with you, asks you questions about another work colleague. Can you answer her using the information given in the box?

     Como se chama ele? ....
     Quantos anos tem? ....
     É casado? ....

Pedro
29
Solteiro

3   Ana and Isabel meet for the first time. You play the part of Isabel (45). Listen to the audio and be guided by it. You need to be able to say:

◆ your name
◆ your age
◆ that you are married
◆ that you have a daughter, Rita

I How would you ask a child his or her age?

2 You want to introduce your mother. Would you use **este é** or **esta é**?

3 If someone is a doctor how would you introduce him?

4 If someone says to you **Quantos anos tem?** how would you answer?

5 What does **ela** mean?

6 If someone asked you **Tem filhos?** what would you answer?

7 Which is the odd one out?

filho   pai   advogado   irmão

8 Can you give the missing numbers in Portuguese?

5, 10, __, 20, __, 30, 35, __

Now check whether you can . . .

- ▨ introduce someone – male or female

- ▨ ask someone how old he/she is, and give your own age

- ▨ say how old someone else is

- ▨ say whether you are married, and ask someone else if he/she is married

- ▨ ask someone if he/she has children, or brothers and sisters, and say what family you have

- ▨ use the numbers 11 to 100

At this early stage you will want to make the most of what you know to answer questions and give information. You can often pick up the words of the questions to form your answer. **É casado/a?** can help you to answer **Sim, sou casado/a**. And **Não, não sou casado/a** will cover separated, divorced and widowed as well as single. You will be surprised how much you can convey with a few words.

4

Um café, por favor

- **ordering a drink in a bar**
- **offering, accepting or refusing**
- **paying for your drinks**
- **using the numbers 100 to 30,000**

Em Portugal . . .

wherever you go you're never far from a **café**. Open from early in the morning until late at night, **cafés** serve all sorts of drinks and food. In some places you have to pay first at the **caixa** (cash desk) and then take your **talão** (receipt) to the **balcão** (counter) where you place your order. The favourite drink is coffee. At any time of the day or night, but especially after a meal, the Portuguese will head for a **café** for their coffee, normally a **bica** (small black coffee).

Ordering a drink . . .

1 Listen to these key phrases.

Faz favor!/Por favor!	Please/Excuse me! (to call the waiter)
Faz favor?	Please/Can I help you?
Um café, por favor	A coffee, please
Uma cerveja, faz favor	A beer, please
De nada	You're welcome

2 Nuno is at Paula's café. What kind of coffee does he order? Use the menu card on the right to help you.

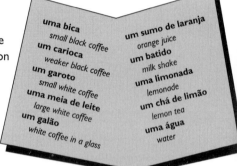

uma bica
small black coffee
um carioca
weaker black coffee
um garoto
small white coffee
uma meia de leite
large white coffee
um galão
white coffee in a glass

um sumo de laranja
orange juice
um batido
milk shake
uma limonada
lemonade
um chá de limão
lemon tea
uma água
water

3 Natália and Alberto arrive and order a beer and a lemonade. Can you say who orders what?

Em português . . .

all nouns (not just those referring to people) are either masculine or feminine and this affects the words for 'a' and 'an'.

um before a masculine noun: **um galão, um café, um sumo**
uma before a feminine noun: **uma cerveja, uma limonada**

Most nouns ending in **-o** are masculine, and most nouns ending in **-a** are feminine. When you come across a new word, try to remember whether it is m. or f.

. . . in a bar

4 Paulo and João both order milk shakes. What flavours do they order?
De here literally means 'of'.

	morango	**baunilha**	**chocolate**
	strawberry	vanilla	chocolate
Paulo	....	....	....
João	....	....	....

5 At the hotel, Senhora Martins and Mr Bryan order some drinks from
the bar. Mr Bryan can't remember the word for wine and he asks
Como se diz em português . . . ? (How do you say in Portuguese?)
What is the word for wine?

*um copo
de vinho*

Barman	**Faz favor?**
Senhora Martins	**Um Martini.**
Mr Bryan	**Uhm . . . Como se diz em português 'wine'?**
Senhora Martins	**Vinho?**
Mr Bryan	**Ah sim, vinho.** **Vinho do Porto, faz favor.**

6 The barman brings the drinks and Mr Bryan thanks him. What does
the barman say?

7 The next day Senhora Martins and Mr Bryan want to try some house
wine (**vinho da casa**). The barman asks them if they want white
(**branco**) or red (**tinto**).

What does each of them want?

Senhora Martins   ....   Mr Bryan   ....

8 How would you order the following?

- a small black coffee, a coffee in a glass and a glass of red wine.

Offering, accepting or refusing

1 Listen to these key phrases.

Que deseja?	What would you like?
Deseja um café?	Would you like a coffee?
Para si?	For you?
Sim, por favor	Yes, please
Não, obrigado	No, thank you
Tchim! Tchim!	Cheers!

2 Paulo asks Senhor Correia and Senhora Pereira what drinks they'd like. Does Senhor Correia want a coffee?

Em português . . .

to make a noun plural the general rule is:
add **-s** for a word ending in **-a/-o/-e**:

um café	**dois cafés**
uma cerveja	**três cervejas**
um batido	**quatro batidos**

add **-es** for a word ending in **-r**:

um bar	**dois bares**

Words ending in **-ão** change in one of three ways – to **-ãos**, **-ões** or **-ães** – and have to be learnt individually. Here is an example:

um galão	**dois galões**

3 Ana orders drinks for her friends. Listen and fill in the gaps. Note how the word 'two' changes for feminine words.

Waiter	**Faz favor?**
Ana	**Dois .... e duas ....**

Tchim! Tchim!

Tchim! Tchim!

Paying for your drinks

1 Listen to some numbers from 100 onwards.

100	**cem**	1000	**mil**	10 000	**dez mil**
200	**duzentos**	2000	**dois mil**	20 000	**vinte mil**
300	**trezentos**	3000	**três mil**	30 000	**trinta mil**
400	**quatrocentos**	4000	**quatro mil**		
500	**quinhentos**	5000	**cinco mil**		
600	**seiscentos**	6000	**seis mil**		
700	**setecentos**	7000	**sete mil**		
800	**oitocentos**	8000	**oito mil**		
900	**novecentos**	9000	**nove mil**		
101	**cento e um**	1100	**mil e cem**		
102	**cento e dois**	1101	**mil cento e um**		
110	**cento e dez**	1135	**mil cento e trinta e cinco**		
	etc.				

Em Portugal . . .

the currency is now the **euro** €. 1 euro = 100 cêntimos. Prices
are usually written with a comma between euros and cêntimos:
   €2   **dois euros**
   €10,25   **dez euros e vinte e cinco**

2 At the café, Paula is telling some of her customers how much their
bills are. Listen and put a tick against the amounts that you hear.

€6,75   €10   €5,50   €1,50

3 To ask how much something is, you say **Quanto é?** Listen to Ana and
João asking how much their bills are and write down the figures.

Ana   **Quanto é?**   *João*   **Quanto é?**
Paula   ....   *Paula*   ....

Put it all together

1 Choose **um** or **uma**. You may need to check the meaning of some of the words in the glossary.

.... **copo de vinho**   .... **gelado**
.... **leite de chocolate**   .... **chá com leite**
.... **limonada**   .... **batido de banana**

Now can you order two of each of them?

dois whiskeys com gelo

duas meias de leite

2 Rearrange the sentences below and build a dialogue between the barman and two customers.

– **Um conhaque.** *(brandy)*
– **E para si?**
– **€2,25.**
– **Faz favor! Que deseja?**
– **Uma cerveja.**
– **Quanto é?**

3 In the café several people have asked for drinks. How much do they come to? Write down the answers.

a a small black coffee?
b a small white coffee and a coffee in a glass?
c a mineral water and a black coffee?
d two orange juices and a small white coffee?

BEBIDAS	
Bica	€0,50
Galão	€0,80
Garoto	€0,60
Sumos	€0,80
Águas	€0,65

Now you're talking!

1   Imagine you're at a café. You are going to order drinks for two
    Portuguese friends and for yourself. The waiter greets you.

   ◇ **Faz favor?**
   ◆ Ask Maria what she'd like to drink.
   ◇ **Um galão, por favor.**
   ◆ Now ask her friend Bernardo what he'd like.
   ◇ **Uma bica, por favor.**
   ◆ At the **caixa** greet the cashier and order a coffee in a glass and two
     black coffees.
   ◆ Ask him how much it is.
   ◇ €**2,60**

2   A friend offers you a coffee.

   ◇ **Deseja um café?**
   ◆ You accept and ask for a large white coffee with milk.

3   Someone asks you what you'd like to drink.

   ◇ **Que deseja?**
   ◆ You ask what 'black coffee' is in Portuguese.

4   Make sure you know the words and phrases for the following
    situation, then close your book and be guided by the recording.

    You have been joined by two friends who'd like some wine. You need
    to be able to:

   ◆ ask your friends what they want to drink
   ◆ ask the waiter for two glasses of wine, one white and one red, and a
     beer for yourself
   ◆ say 'Thank you' when the waiter comes back
   ◆ say 'Cheers!'

Quiz

1. What are the two ways of saying 'please' in Portuguese?
2. The waiter says **Faz favor?** What is he asking you to do?
3. How would you ask someone how to say 'vanilla' in Portuguese?
4. Would you use **um** or **uma** with the following?

   .... **sumo**   .... **cerveja**   .... **bica**   .... **copo de vinho**
5. Someone has bought you a drink. Say 'Cheers!'
6. Order two of each of the following:

   um galão, uma água, uma bica
7. How would you ask your colleague if he/she wants a coffee?
8. Say the following amounts in Portuguese:

   €5,80   €4,55   €1,67   €11,90.
9. What is the difference between **um garoto, uma meia de leite** and **um galão**?

Now check whether you can . . .

- order a drink in a bar

- offer someone a drink

- accept when someone offers you a drink or refuse politely

- ask what something is in Portuguese

- say 'Cheers!'

Now try and increase your vocabulary by looking up in the dictionary any drinks that you and your friends or family like. Wherever you go, look out for new words and write them down in your notebook. Try also to remember whether they are masculine or feminine. Before you order any drinks, make a mental list in Portuguese of what you want.

Ponto de controle 1

1 Listen as Paula de Oliveira chats to one of her customers, Arlete Cardoso, and then tick the right information.

a	**É**	portuguesa	italiana
b	**É de**	Braga	Faro
c	**É**	pintora	professora
d	**É**	solteira	casada
e	**Tem**	uma filha	um filho
f	**O filho/A filha tem**	treze anos	quinze anos

2 Two students of Portuguese are getting to know each other. Listen to their conversation and fill in the grid:

nome	nacionalidade	profissão
Rita	....	....
Carlos	....	....

3 They decide to have a drink together at the Bar Central after their class. Listen and note what they each order.

	bebida (drink)
Rita	....
Carlos	....

4 Rita and Carlos hear Paula telling three other clients what their bills are. Listen to Paula saying the prices and write down the amounts.

Um copo de vinho tinto　　.....................
Um copo de leite　　.....................
Um sumo de laranja natural　.....................

5 Can you say the plural of these words?

Bebidas (drinks)

bica
limonada
galão
sumo de ananás

Profissões (professions)

professor
estudante
escritor
jornalista

Now check your pronunciation with the audio.

6 In activity 5 all the occupations were in the masculine form. If the people doing these same jobs were women, what would they say?

Check your answers with the audio.

7 You're in the hotel bar with some other students of Portuguese and you've been asked to order the drinks. To find out what the others want, you'll need to rearrange the words. The clues will help you.

a	A type of coffee	TOORGA MU
b	An alcoholic drink	QUENHOCA MU
c	A type of water	GÁUA MAU
d	A drink made with milk	ODTIBA MU

Now call the waiter and place the order. Don't forget to order something for yourself!

8 Renata is Marta's new penfriend from Hamburg. How would she introduce herself and her family? Choose the correct option to complete each sentence.

a **Chamo-me/Chama-se Renata. Sou alemã, de Hamburgo.**
b **Tem/Tenho 15 anos.**
c **Tem/Tenho 2 irmãos, o Hanz de 17 anos e o Franz de 20 anos.**
d **O meu/A minha pai é advogado.**
e **O meu/A minha mãe é professora de inglês.**

9 Three people introduce themselves at a language school. Fill in the gaps using the words in the box on the right:

Pierre   **Bom dia. Eu sou .... Pierre Larousse.**

Ilda   **Ilda Rosas. Muito prazer. ....
é a Teresa.**

Teresa **..................·**

Pierre   **Eu .... de Lion em França.
E você, ... é?**

Ilda   **Eu sou de Madrid. A Teresa ....
de Valencia.**

> o
> é
> esta
> donde
> Muito prazer
> sou

10 Which is the odd one out?

a **bebidas:**
batido, galão, cerveja, baunilha

b **nacionalidades:**
francês, galês, italiana, solteiro

c **família:**
alemão, filho, irmã, mãe

d **números:**
vinte, anos, novecentos, mil

11 Match up one word from column A with another from column B to make a Portuguese phrase.

A	B
a **É**	**si?**
b **Tudo**	**inglês.**
c **Para**	**casado?**
d **Sou**	**faz?**
e **O que**	**bem?**

12 Paula Ferreira's sister wants to apply for a job in England. She asks for your help in filling in a form with her personal details. What questions would you ask her to find out her name, where she is from, her age, her occupation and her phone number?

a ....

b ....

c ....

d ....

e ....

13 Paulo introduces himself and his family. Read the text then say if each of the statements underneath is **verdadeiro** or **falso**.

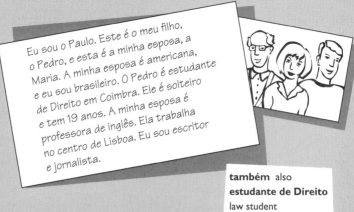

Eu sou o Paulo. Este é o meu filho, o Pedro, e esta é a minha esposa, a Maria. A minha esposa é americana, e eu sou brasileiro. O Pedro é estudante de Direito em Coimbra. Ele é solteiro e tem 19 anos. A minha esposa é professora de inglês. Ela trabalha no centro de Lisboa. Eu sou escritor e jornalista.

também also
estudante de Direito law student

	verdadeiro	falso
a Pedro is Paulo's father	☐	☐
b Pedro is not married	☐	☐
c They are all Brazilian	☐	☐
d Maria is Paulo's daughter	☐	☐
e Maria is a teacher	☐	☐
f Paulo is a writer	☐	☐

5

CINCO

Desculpe, onde é a estação?

- asking where something is
- asking for help with the answer
- talking about where you live and work

Em Portugal . . .

old towns with their narrow streets and romantic little squares are the focus of attraction for many visitors.

History is all around you and is particularly evident in the names of **ruas** (streets) and **praças** (squares), which often commemorate famous people: **a Rua Garrett** (Garrett Street, after a writer), **a Avenida Infante Dom Henrique** (after Henry the Navigator) or historical events: **a Praça dos Restauradores** (Restauradores Square, after the rising of 1 December 1640 which put an end to 60 years of Spanish rule).

Asking where something is . . .

1 Listen to these key phrases.

Onde é . . . ?	Where is . . . ?/Where is it?
Onde é a estação?	Where is the station?
É longe?	Is it far?
. . . cinco minutos a pé	. . . five minute walk

2 Steve has just arrived in the city and his friend Maria is pointing out certain landmarks on the map for him. Look at the map and check the meanings of the words.

Now listen and match the places with the phrases below.

a **é aqui** (here) *b* **é na rua Augusta** (Augusta street)
c **é ali** (there) *d* **é no centro da cidade** (city centre)
e **é perto** (nearby)

Em português . . .

the words for 'the' in the singular are:
o before a masculine noun

o banco (bank)	**o hospital** (hospital)
o museu (museum)	**o jardim** (garden)

a before a feminine noun

a loja (shop)	**a estação** (station)
a rua (street)	**a praça** (square)

. . . and asking for help with the answer

3 Listen to these key phrases.

Onde são . . . ?	Where are . . . ?
Onde são as lojas?	Where are the shops?
Pode repetir, por favor?	Can you repeat that, please?
Pode falar devagar?	Can you speak slowly?
a quinhentos metros daqui	500 metres away
entre . . . e . . .	between . . . and . . .

4 Steve wants to know where the shops are. How does he ask? Does he understand the reply? How far is it to the shops? Fill in the gaps.

Steve   **Desculpe, ... as lojas?**
Passer-by   **As lojas? A .... metros daqui.**
Steve   **.............................?**
Passer-by   **............................. Dez minutos a pé.**

5 Next he looks for the bank and again asks for directions. Does he understand what he is told? Can you fill in the details for him?

Passer-by   **É ali, entre .... e ....**

6 Later, he wants to visit **o castelo** (the castle), and asks a passer-by where it is. How far away is it? How long will it take to get there?

7 How would you ask where the following are?
● the bank   ● Augusta Street   ● the ruins

Em português . . .

in the plural, the words for 'the' are:

os	**os bancos**	**os museus**
as	**as lojas**	**as ruínas**

Talking about where you live . . .

1   Listen to these key phrases.

Onde mora?   Where do you live?
(Eu) moro em Faro   I live in Faro
   . . . na rua do Alecrim   . . . in Alecrim Street
   . . . no centro   . . . in the centre
   . . . no campo   . . . in the country

2   Listen to Carlos as he asks Maria and some of her friends where they
live. Fill in the gaps.

Carlos   **Onde mora, Maria?**
Maria   **Moro em Faro, no .... de Faro,**
              .... do Alecrim.
Carlos   **E você, Isabel?**
Isabel   **Eu moro na Praia da Luz.**
Paulo   **Eu moro no ...., a 30 quilómetros de Lagos.**

Em português . . .

to say where you live, you can sometimes just use **em** + place:
   Moro em Lisboa   **Moro em Londres**
If you need to be more specific, you use **em** + **o** or **a**:
em + **o** = **no**   **Moro no centro**
em + **a** = **na**   **Moro na rua Garrett**
When a place owes its name to a physical feature, you put **o** or **a**
before it:
   o Porto   **Oporto** (**porto** = harbour)
   a Ilha da Madeira   **Madeira** (**ilha** = island)
   a Praia da Figueira   (**praia** = beach)
This affects how you say you live in it:
   Moro no Porto   **Moro na Praia da Figueira**

---

3   How would you say you live in the following places?

- Dublin   • the city centre   • King Street

. . . and work

4   Listen to these key phrases.

Onde trabalha?	Where do you work?
Trabalho . . .	I work . . .
. . . num escritório	. . . in an office
. . . num colégio	. . . in a college
. . . numa loja	. . . in a shop

'In a' or 'in an' . . . is **num** before a masculine noun, **numa** before a feminine noun.

5   Carlos now asks his three friends where they work. Listen and tick their workplaces.

	num escritório	numa loja	num banco
Maria	▨	▨	▨
Paulo	▨	▨	▨
Isabel	▨	▨	▨

Where does Carlos say he works?
How does Maria say she works in a bank?

Em português . . .

to show who is doing something, you change the ending of the verb. You occasionally need the words for 'I', 'you', 'he' etc. for clarity or emphasis:

		morar (to live)	**trabalhar** (to work)
(eu)	I	**moro**	**trabalho**
(tu)	you	**moras**	**trabalhas** (informal)
você	you	**mora**	**trabalha**
ele/ela	he/she	**mora**	**trabalha**

To say something negative you simply put **não** before the verb.

Put it all together

1 Do you know which words to use for 'the'?

a	..... centro	..... rua	..... praça
b	..... escritório	..... loja	..... colégio
c	..... castelo	..... estação	..... museu
d	..... porto	..... praia	..... ilha

2 Choose a verb from the box and fill in the blanks.

a **Pode** .... **devagar?**
b **Pode** ....?
c **Onde** .... **o centro?**
d **Onde** .... **o Fernando?**
e **Onde** .... **os restaurantes?**
f **Não** ....
g .... **numa loja?**

é
mora
são
repetir
falar
trabalhas
trabalho

3 What question would you ask if:

a you want to know where the beach is?
b you haven't understood what somebody has said?
c you want to know where someone lives?
d and where someone works?

Onde mora?

Onde é a praia?

Pode repetir, por favor?

Onde trabalha?

4 Can you insert the correct words for 'in' to say where Ana lives and works?

a .... **Cascais**
b .... **centro de Lisboa**
c .... **rua Augusta**
d .... **escritório**

Now you're talking!

1   You're at Paula's café planning your day. Paula comes over to speak
    to you.

   ◇ **Olá, bom dia.**
   ◆ Greet her and ask her where the cathedral is.
   ◇ **A catedral é na rua de São Miguel.**
   ◆ Ask her where São Miguel Street is.
   ◇ **É aqui.** (She points it out on the map)
   ◆ Ask her if it is far.
   ◇ **Não. É a 200 metros daqui.**
   ◆ Thank her and say goodbye.

2   Another customer comes in, sits down at your table and starts talking
    to you. He suggests somewhere for you to visit.

   ◇ **O Museu da Marinha.**
   ◆ You didn't quite catch what he said. Ask him to repeat it.
   ◇ **O Museu da Marinha. É entre o mosteiro e o jardim
      botânico. Não é longe … a cinco minutos a pé.**
   ◆ Thank him and repeat where he says the museum is.

3   He asks you some questions. You might like to prepare your answers
    and then be guided by the audio. You'll need to be able to say:

   ◆ your name, your nationality, and the town you live in
   ◆ if you have a job, what you do and where you work

4   You'd like to know more about him.

   ◆ Ask where he lives.
   ◇ **Moro no campo.**
   ◆ Ask him if it's far.
   ◇ **Não é longe … a vinte quilómetros daqui.**

Quiz

1 How would you say: 'I live in Brighton and I work in London'?
2 You're lost. How would you ask where the city centre is?
3 Someone says **Não trabalho.** What do they mean?
4 Would you use **em**, **no** or **na** with **Porto** to say 'I live in Oporto'?
5 How would you ask someone where they live?
6 How would you ask someone to repeat something?
7 Make a sentence with these words:
   ele, **Liberdade**, **Avenida**, **trabalha**, **da**, **na**

Now check whether you can . . .

■ ask where something is

■ ask if it is far

■ ask someone to repeat something

■ ask someone where they live and work

■ say where you live and work

Language follows patterns, and understanding these patterns helps you use new words correctly and build up new sentences related to what you want to say. Many verbs ending in **-ar**, such as **falar** (to speak), follow the same pattern as **morar** and **trabalhar** (see page 47). So, if you want to say 'I speak Portuguese', you say **Falo português**, and if you want to say 'I don't speak German', you say **Não falo alemão**. Words for languages are the same as the masculine nationalities on page 17.

Now can you say which languages you speak?

Há um banco aqui perto?

- **finding out what there is in town**
- **. . . and when it's open**
- **making simple enquiries**
- **understanding directions**

Em Portugal . . .

an early visit to the local tourist information office (**o Centro de Turismo**) will be worthwhile if you want to know what to see in a town or city. You'll be given **uma planta da cidade** (a map of the city), **folhetos** (leaflets) and information about local places of interest, and perhaps also a list of forthcoming events in the region.

As well as the main cities such as Faro, Lisbon, Oporto, Braga and Viana do Castelo, there are many pleasant small towns and villages with spectacular views and interesting things to see. If you have time, go for a tour of the green and mountainous north and then contrast it with the flatter and more arid south.

Finding out what there is in town . . .

I Listen to these key phrases.

Aqui é . . .	Here's . . .
Há . . .	Is there . . .
. . . uma piscina?	. . . a swimming pool?
Há . . .	There is/There are . . .
Não há . . .	There isn't/There aren't . . .
na parte nova	in the new part
na parte velha	in the old part

2 Can you match these Portuguese words with their English equivalents? Look up any you can't guess in the glossary.

language school
baker's
museum
chemist's
swimming pool
library
supermarket
post office

a	**um supermercado**	*b*	**uma biblioteca**
c	**um museu**	*d*	**uma padaria**
e	**um correio**	*f*	**uma piscina**
g	**uma escola de línguas**	*h*	**uma farmácia**

3 To find out what there is in town, Carlos goes to the **Centro de Turismo** where he talks to the assistant, Madalena Fernandes. He asks her about several places in the list above. Can you tick them as you hear them? Now answer the following questions:

		Sim	Não
a	**Há uma escola de línguas?**		
b	**Há um museu?**		
c	**Há um supermercado?**		
d	**Há uma piscina?**		

4 How would you ask the following questions:

- is there a chemist's?
- is there a post office?

. . . and when it's open

5 Listen to these key phrases.

Está aberto/aberta	It's open
Está fechado/fechada	It's closed
. . . todos os dias	. . . every day
. . . aos domingos	. . . on Sundays
. . . às quintas-feiras	. . . on Thursdays

- **segunda-feira** (Mon)   **quinta-feira** (Thurs)
- **terça-feira** (Tue)   **sexta-feira** (Fri)
- **quarta-feira** (Wed)   **sábado** (Sat)
- **domingo** (Sun)

6 Madalena is telling Carlos what days the swimming pool and the museum are open or closed, and when there is **um mercado** (a market). Listen and fill in the gaps.

- **A piscina está aberta** ....·
- **O museu está fechado aos** .... **e aos** ....·
- **Há um mercado às** ....·

Em português . . .

when describing places or objects (just as with people), adjectives have to be masculine or feminine to agree with what they describe.
A loja está aberta   **O banco está aberto**

7 How would you ask if the following places are open every day?

- the bank   ● the supermarket   ● the baker's

Now ask if the supermarket is closed on Sundays.

Making simple enquiries . . .

1   Listen to these key phrases.

Há um banco aqui perto?   Is there a bank near here?
Peço desculpa   I'm sorry
Não sei   I don't know
ao fundo   at the end

sempre em frente

à esquerda   **à direita**

2   After visiting the Museu de Arte Antiga, Carlos wants to find **a casa de banho** (toilet), and he asks a museum official. Where does she say it is? Tick the right expressions as you hear them.

alí ao fundo   **à esquerda**
sempre em frente   **à direita**

3   Outside in the street he looks for a telephone, and stops somebody to ask if there's one nearby. How does he ask? Does the person know the answer?

4   He stops another person to ask the same question and this time he is in luck. What is he told?

Listen out for **depois** (then) and fill in the blanks:

..................., **depois à** ....

5   He also asks this person whether there is a bank in the area. Listen out for **na primeira rua à direita** (the first street on the right).

Can you write down in English the instructions he is given?

. . . and understanding directions

6   Listen to these key phrases.

A paragem do autocarro	The bus stop
é antes/depois . . .	is before/after . . .
. . . do banco/da estação	. . . the bank/the station
É em frente . . .	It's opposite . . .
. . . do hotel/da farmácia	. . . the hotel/the chemist's

7   Carlos and Isabel decide to visit the castle and they ask a passer-by for
    directions. Where is it? How long would it take to walk there?
    Where's the bus stop?

8   From the castle they look down towards the town and see some of
    the places they still want to visit. Listen and tick whether each of the
    following is **verdadeiro** or **falso**:

		V	**F**
a	**O teatro é em frente do museu.**		
b	**O mosteiro é alí à esquerda.**		
c	**A piscina é em frente da praia.**		

Em português . . .

when talking about the position of things
a often means 'at' or 'on':

    a + **o** becomes **ao**   <u>ao</u> **fundo**
    a + **a** becomes **à**   <u>à</u> **esquerda**, <u>à</u> **direita**

de often means 'of' or 'to':

    de + **o** becomes **do**   **em frente <u>do</u> hotel**
    de + **a** becomes **da**   **em frente <u>da</u> praia**

Put it all together

1 Read the following notices then answer the questions.

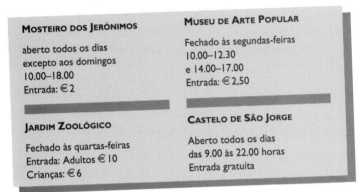

Mosteiro dos Jerónimos

aberto todos os dias
excepto aos domingos
10.00–18.00
Entrada: €2

Museu de Arte Popular

Fechado às segundas-feiras
10.00–12.30
e 14.00–17.00
Entrada: €2,50

Jardim Zoológico

Fechado às quartas-feiras
Entrada: Adultos €10
Crianças: €6

Castelo de São Jorge

Aberto todos os dias
das 9.00 às 22.00 horas
Entrada gratuita

a Is the monastery open every day?
b When is the zoo closed?
c When is the museum closed?
d Is entrance to the castle free?

2 Can you say where these buildings are in relation to you, if you are standing at the entrance to the square?

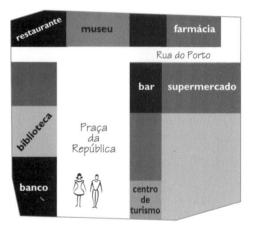

a **O Centro de Turismo é aqui à** ....**.**
b **O supermercado é na** ...., **à** ....**.**
c **A farmácia é** .... **supermercado.**
d **O restaurante é** ...., **à** ....**.**

Now you're talking!

1   Imagine that you have just landed at Lisbon airport on a Monday morning and you need to change some money. You go to the information desk . . .

   ◇ **Bom dia.**
   ◆ Say hello and ask if there is a bank nearby.
   ◇ **Sim, há um em frente do café.**
   ◆ Also ask if there is a chemist's nearby.
   ◇ **Sim, a farmácia é aqui em frente.**
   ◆ And ask where the toilet is.
   ◇ **É aqui ao fundo à direita.**

2   You are now at the hotel.

   ◆ Ask the receptionist if there is a tourist office in the old part of the city.
   ◇ **Sim, há um na segunda rua à esquerda.**
   ◆ Repeat the instructions and thank her.

3   At the tourist office an assistant greets you and gives you a map.

   ◇ **Faz favor, uma planta da cidade.**
   ◆ Thank her and ask where the museum is.
   ◇ **Na primeira rua à esquerda.**
   ◆ Repeat the instructions. Then ask her if it's open today.
   ◇ **Sim, está aberto todos os dias.**
   ◆ Now ask where the castle is.
   ◇ **Aqui é o castelo e aqui é a paragem do autocarro número 43.**
   ◆ Ask if it is before the museum.
   ◇ **Não, a paragem é depois do museu.**
   ◆ Ask if the castle is open on Mondays.
   ◇ **Não o castelo está fechado às segundas-feiras.**

Quiz

1. How would you ask if there is a café nearby?
2. If a shop is open, would it say **aberta** or **fechada**?
3. Which way would you go if someone says to you:
   Sempre em frente, depois na primeira à esquerda?
4. What day of the week is **terça-feira**?
5. How would you say 'I'm sorry. I don't know'?
6. Which is the odd one out?
   biblioteca, castelo, rua, piscina, teatro
7. If you are told that there is a market **às sextas-feiras**, does it mean on Thursdays or Fridays?
8. How would you say 'I don't work on Sundays'?

Now check whether you can . . .

- ask and say what there is in a town
- ask if a place is open or closed
- recognise the days of the week
- say you're sorry
- say you don't know
- understand some straightforward directions
- understand where one place is in relation to another

You could practise the names of places and their relative positions by imagining that you are telling a Portuguese person about your home town. You could tell him what there is (e.g. museum, swimming pool), point them out on a map and say when they're open.

In Units 5 and 6 we have met several little words such as **ao**, **à**, **na**, **do**, **numa**, **aos**, which are quite difficult to get right. Don't worry about making mistakes at this stage – they will all come right with practice!

Quanto custa?

- **asking and understanding the price**
- **describing and commenting**
- **buying food in a shop or market**

Em Portugal . . .

there is a great variety of places to shop: markets where you can buy fresh food, clothes, pottery, flowers, etc; small shops selling modest and traditional items, and modern shops and boutiques selling designer clothes. Usually shops are open from 9.30 a.m. until 7.30 p.m. Many close for lunch between 1.00 and 3.00 p.m.

In a **tabacaria** (tobacconist's shop), and often in a **quiosque** (street kiosk) as well, you'll find newspapers, magazines, postcards, cigarettes and sweets. In a **quiosque** you can also buy **bilhetes de autocarro/eléctrico** (bus/tram tickets). To buy stamps you go to a post office or find a stamp vending machine.

Asking and understanding the price

I Listen to these key phrases.

Diga	Can I help you?
Tem . . . ?	Have you got . . . ?
Quanto custa?	How much is it?
Quanto custa tudo?	How much is everything?
Quanto custam?	How much are they?
50 cêntimos cada	50 cents each

2 Listen as Manuela buys **uma revista** (a magazine), **um jornal**
(a newspaper) and some **postais** (postcards) in a **tabacaria**. First fill
in the blanks with **custa** or **custam**, then listen again and fill in
the prices.

- **Bom dia. Diga.**
- **Quanto .... a revista?**   € ....
- **E quanto .... o jornal?**   € ....
- **Os postais quanto ....?**   € ....

How much is the total cost?   € ....

Em português . . .

nouns ending in **-al** change to **-ais** in the plural:

um postal	**dois postais**
um jornal	**dois jornais**

---

3 In the post office she buys **selos** (stamps) **para a União Européia**
(for the EU) and **um cartão telefónico** (phone card). How does she
ask what the stamps cost? And the phone card?
What is the cost of the stamps and phone card together?

4 Now can you ask how much the following cost?

- **quatro selos**   • **uma revista**   • **dois postais**

Describing and commenting

I   Listen to these key phrases.

É demasiado . . .	It's too . . .
. . . caro/a	. . . expensive
. . . pequeno/a	. . . small
. . . grande	. . . big
Levo . . .	I'll take . . .

2   Carlos and Isabel decide to have a look at the market. Listen to their conversation and put a tick against the items you hear.

um saco de desporto
  sports bag
um livro book
uma T-shirt T-shirt
sapatos shoes

3   Listen to the recording again. What does she say about the **saco de desporto**? How does she say she'll take the T-shirt?

Em português . . .

adjectives ending in **-o** change to **-a** when used with feminine nouns:

| m. | **caro** | **o livro é caro** |
| f. | **cara** | **a T-shirt é cara** |

Adjectives ending in **-e** do not change in the feminine:

    o livro é grande   **a T-shirt é grande**

Most adjectives add **-s** when used with plural nouns:

    os livros são caros   **as T-shirts são grandes**

Note that **demasiado** does not change its ending.

4   How would you say the following?

- The magazine is expensive.
- The T-shirt is too small.
- The book is too expensive.
- It's too big!

Buying food in a shop . . .

trezentos gramas

meio litro   um litro   meio quilo   um quilo

1 Isabel needs to buy food. First read her list
and look up any words you don't know.
Now listen and tick each item as she says it.
Which one does she forget to write down?

**um pão
de
forma**

uma garrafa de
vinho tinto
uma garrafa de
água mineral
dois pães de forma
um quilo de açúcar
meio quilo de queijo
300 gramas de
fiambre

2 Listen to these key phrases.

Dê-me . . .	Could you give me . . .
Queria . . .	I'd like . . .
Mais alguma coisa?	Anything else?
É só	That's all

3 Isabel remembers two more items she wants to buy. Listen and fill in
how much of each she asks for (**uma lata** is a can).

– **Dê-me** .... de café, por favor.
– **Também queria** .... de tomates.

. . . or market

bananas | pêssegos | cogumelos | cebolas | maçãs | morangos | batatas | tomates

4 In the market Isabel goes to the **banca da fruta e verdura** (fruit and vegetable stall). Which fruit does she ask for?

peaches   strawberries   apples   bananas

5 Next she asks for some **verdura** (vegetables). Listen and fill in the quantities she buys of each.

.... **batatas**   .... **cebolas**   .... **tomates**

6 She sees the **banca do peixe** (fish stall) and decides to go over for a closer look. What sort of fish does she ask about? What does she decide to buy and why?

> **o bacalhau** cod
> **o peixe espada** swordfish
> **a sardinha** sardine

Isabel	**Quanto custa o ....?**
Empregada	**€10 o quilo.**
Isabel	**Ah, é demasiado caro!**
	...., faz favor.

7 *a* Can you ask how much the following cost?

- the newspaper   ● the bottle of wine   ● the strawberries

b Can you ask for the following in a shop?

- 1/2 kg of ham   ● 250 g of cheese   ● a tin of tomatoes

Put it all together

1   Can you match the English with the Portuguese phrases?

    a   **Tem?**   How much is it?
    b   **É só**   Could you give me
    c   **É demasiado caro**   How much are they?
    d   **Dê-me**   Do you have?
    e   **Quanto custa?**   It's too expensive
    f   **Mais alguma coisa?**   That's all
    g   **Quanto custam?**   Anything else?

2   Where would you buy the following products? Put each one in the correct column.

maçãs, selos, queijo, morangos, postais, sardinhas, bacalhau, pêssegos, jornal, fiambre, açúcar, peixe espada.

banca da fruta	banca do peixe	tabacaria	supermercado
....	....	....	....
....	....	....	....
....	....	....	....

3   Maria is going to the market. Can you help her write her shopping list in Portuguese? She needs the following:

1 kilo of potatoes, 400 grams of ham, 3 kilos of onions,
½ kilo of cheese, 1 bottle of white wine

4   These items at the supermarket cost you the following amounts in **euros** and **cêntimos**. What are they in figures?

    a   **pão:**   **cinquenta e nove cêntimos**   ....
    b   **queijo:**   **nove euros e quarenta e sete**   ....
    c   **fiambre:**   **um euro e setenta e oito**   ....
    d   Now add them up and give the total in words and figures.

Now you're talking!

1   You're having a party and you need to buy a few items. First you go to the **loja das bebidas** (drinks shop).

     ◇ **Bom dia. Diga.**
     ◆ Ask for twelve bottles of white wine and six bottles of red wine.
     ◇ **Mais alguma coisa?**
     ◆ Ask for three bottles of mineral water.
     ◇ **É só?**
     ◆ Ask for twelve bottles of beer.
     ◇ **Cerveja Sagres?**
     ◆ Say Yes and ask how much it is in total.

2   Next you go to the **charcutaria** (delicatessen).

     ◆ Ask if they have any ham.
     ◇ **Sim, quanto?**
     ◆ Ask for 300 grams.
     ◇ **Aqui está. Mais alguma coisa?**
     ◆ Say you'd like half a kilo of cheese.
     ◇ **É só?**
     ◆ Say that's all, and ask how much it all is.

3   Then you go to the **correio** (post office).

     ◆ Ask how much a stamp for America costs.
     ◇ €**0,70.**
     ◆ Ask for three stamps, and say you'd like three postcards as well.
     ◇ **Três postais . . .**
     ◆ Ask how much everything is.
     ◇ €**3,10.**

Quiz

1 Would you use **Quanto custa?** or **Quanto custam?** to ask how much the following cost?
    as bananas, o gelado, os selos, o jornal
2 How would you ask how much a stamp costs?
3 How would you say 'It's too expensive' when referring to a magazine?
4 What is **um quilo de pêssegos**?
5 Are the following vegetables or fruit?
    batatas, **cebolas**, **cogumelos**?
6 What can you buy in **a banca do peixe**?
7 How would you say 'I'd like three bottles of mineral water'?
8 Which word do you need to insert to say 'It's too small'?
    É .... **pequeno**

Now check whether you can . . .

■ ask how much something costs

■ understand the answer

■ say you'd like something

■ comment on or describe something simply

■ give some details of what you want to buy, e.g.
    ask for a kilo, half a kilo, 100 grams of food
    ask for a bottle, a litre, half a litre of a liquid
    ask for stamps for a particular country

Looking up a word in an English–Portuguese dictionary can be complicated because there is often more than one translation given. To find the correct meaning it's often helpful to bear in mind the context in which the word appears. You can always check what you think the word is in Portuguese is by looking it up again in a Portuguese–English dictionary.

Ponto de controle 2

1 Steve Llewellyn and Maria Fernandes are looking for the **Clube de Desporto** (sports club) where they are to meet Carlos and Isabel. They ask a passer-by for directions. Listen and then answer these questions:

a Where is the sports centre? ....

b How far is it?   ....

c What directions are they given?

....

2 At the sports club Carlos tells them what facilities there are and when it is open.

a What facilities are available?
   piscina   restaurante   parque   café
   sauna   campo de ténis   loja   ginásio

b Is the club open every day?

3 Steve and Maria look round the sports club and decide they would like to join. At the reception desk they are given application forms to fill in. Listen as they discuss the details and fill in Maria's form.

CLUBE DE DESPORTO DO SPORTING	
Nome:	Maria Fernandes
Morada (address):	Rua Almirante Reis No.
Telefone:	....
Idade (age):	....
Altura (height):	.... metros
Peso (weight):	.... quilos

4 Maria and Steve have a look round the sports shop. Which of these do they buy? Look up any words you don't know.

fato de treino   **calções**   **T-shirt**

sapatos de treino   **saco de desporto**

5 Listen to the conversation in the shop again and answer these questions:

a How much does the tracksuit cost?
b What do they say about it?
c How much are the T-shirts?
d What size T-shirt does Steve need?

     tamanho pequeno (small)   ▬
     tamanho médio (medium)   ▬
     tamanho grande (large)   ▬

e What do they decide to buy?

6 Maria decides to pay for her shopping by cheque. Can you write down the total amount in words and figures?

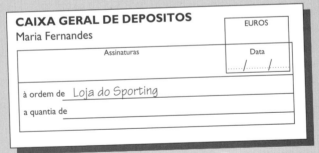

CAIXA GERAL DE DEPOSITOS	EUROS
Maria Fernandes	
Assinaturas	Data
	...../....../.....
à ordem de Loja do Sporting	
a quantia de	

7 Later in the day, Maria goes to the supermarket with Steve to buy some food. Maria likes vegetables and fish but won't eat meat. Which of the following do you think she'll buy?

três tomates grandes
200 gramas de fiambre
cinco maçãs
quatro quilos de batatas
um quilo de bacalhau
quatro hamburguers
meio quilo de cogumelos

8 She also needs some drinks. Match the two columns to find out the exact items.

a **vinho** **natural**
b **água** **de chocolate**
c **café** **mineral**
d **leite** **descafeinado**
e **sumo** **tinto**

9 After the supermarket they go to the **papelaria** (stationer's). Fill in the blanks using the words from the box.

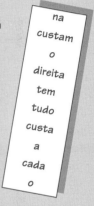

na
custam
o
direita
tem
tudo
custa
a
cada
o

Maria	**Quanto .... o livro?**
Empregado	**€ 22,50.**
Maria	**Quanto .... os postais?**
Empregado	**€ 1,25 ....**
Maria	**................. selos?**
Empregado	**Não. O correio é ....**
	primeira rua à ....
Maria	**Quanto custa ....?**
Empregado	**................. livro, ... jornal,**
	cinco postais e .... revista:
	€ 32,30.

10 Can you write the questions to the answers given below?

a **Moro em Coimbra.**
b **Um banco? Sim. Há um na segunda rua à esquerda.**
c **O Centro de Turismo é na praça.**
d **Não, não é longe.**
e **Trabalho num escritório.**

11 Maria and Steve plan to go to a Chinese restaurant for lunch, to the cinema in the evening and then to a nightclub. Carlos writes down some directions. Which letter on the map corresponds to:

a the restaurant? *b* the cinema? *c* the nightclub?

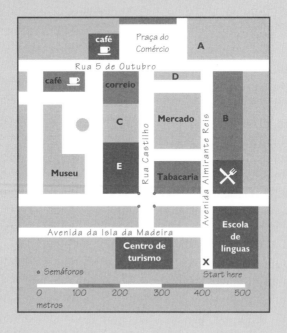

> Há um restaurante chinês no centro da cidade, na rua Castilho. É na primeira rua à esquerda, depois na primeira à direita. O restaurante é à esquerda, em frente do mercado. O cinema é sempre em frente, ao fundo da avenida Almirante Reis. A discoteca é em frente do cinema, na rua 5 de Outubro.

8

Queria um quarto

- checking in at a hotel
- finding a hotel room
- booking ahead by phone
- making requests

Em Portugal . . .

accommodation is usually quite easy to find. Places to stay include simple and inexpensive 1-star hotels and **casas de hóspedes** (guest houses), **pensões** (boarding houses), luxurious 4- and 5-star hotels, and **pousadas** (state-owned hotels, mostly in the country) which are usually very well managed and equipped. **Estalagens** (inns) are similar to **pousadas** but are also found in towns. **Pousadas de juventude** (youth hostels) offer accommodation at budget prices but there are relatively few of them. When booking a room always check if breakfast is included in the price: **o pequeno almoço está incluído?**

Checking in at a hotel

1 Listen to these key phrases.

Reservei . . . I've booked . . .

. . . um quarto simples

. . . um quarto com duas camas

. . . um quarto de casal

. . . com banho

. . . com duche

no terceiro piso on the third floor
no segundo piso on the second floor
no primeiro piso on the first floor
no rés-do-chão (R/C) on the ground floor

O seu nome? Your name?
O seu passaporte, por favor Your passport, please

2 Margarida Pinto is the receptionist at the Hotel Central. Several guests
arrive and check in. Listen as she greets them and checks their names
in the register, before giving them their key (**a chave**). Listen several
times, then fill in the details on the grid.

	tipo de quarto	banho/ duche	número de quarto	piso
Sr Lopes	....	....	....	....
Sra Fortes	....	....	....	....
Sr Abreu	....	....	....	....

3 Listen to Margarida again and make a note of where the lift
(**o elevador**) is.

Finding a hotel room

1 Listen to these key phrases.

Tem um quarto?   Do you have a room?
para uma noite   for one night
para esta noite   for tonight
Como se escreve?   How do you spell it?

2 A couple arrive at reception and ask Margarida for a room. What kind of rooms do they want?
How long do they want to stay?
What room numbers are they offered?

3 Now listen to Margarida saying the Portuguese alphabet and repeat it.

A B C D E F G H I J L M N O P Q R S T U V X Z

Which English letters do not feature in the Portuguese alphabet?

4 Margarida asks the couple to spell their surnames. Circle the correct words below.

Gonzalez   **Gonçalves**   **Martim**   **Martins**

5 Margarida is spelling some hotel names for Steve. Listen to their conversation and fill in the spaces below.

HOTEL   _ _ **LA**_ _ _ **RA**
POUSADA   _**O**_ **VA**_ _**O**
Try spelling your name and that of your home town.

6 How would you ask if the hotel has:

● a double room with shower?   ● a single room with bath?

Booking ahead by phone

1 Listen to these key phrases.

Estou	Hello (on the phone)
Queria um quarto	I'd like a room
Para quando?	When for?
Para quantas noites?	For how many nights?
Para duas semanas	For two weeks
Um momento	One moment
Não há vagas	There are no vacancies
Está bem	OK, that's fine

Janeiro January	**Fevereiro** February	**Março** March	**Abril** April
Maio May	**Junho** June	**Julho** July	**Agosto** August
Setembro September	**Outubro** October	**Novembro** November	**Dezembro** December

Em português . . .

dates are expressed with the number + **de** + month:

um de Julho	1st July
vinte e sete de Setembro	27th September
para um de Fevereiro	for 1st of February
de trinta de Junho . . .	from 30th June . . .
. . . a treze de Julho	. . . to 13th July
dia cinco	the 5th (day)

2 Margarida is taking some bookings over the phone. Listen and decide what dates these people want rooms for.

a .... *b* .... *c* ....

Making requests

1 Listen to these key phrases.

Posso . . . /Podemos . . .	Can I . . . /Can we . . .
. . . telefonar daqui?	. . . phone from here?
. . . comprar selos?	. . . buy stamps?
. . . estacionar aqui?	. . . park here?
. . . nadar na piscina?	. . . swim in the pool?
O telefone não trabalha	The phone isn't working

Em português . . .

the verb which follows **posso/podemos** is always in the infinitive (the form which you find in the dictionary, ending in **-ar, -er** or **-ir**).

The infinitives on this page all end in **-ar**:
telefonar = to phone   **comprar** = to buy

2 Four hotel guests ask at reception if they can do certain things. Answer **Sim** or **Não** in each case.

What does Margarida say about the phone and the pool?

3 A couple arrive at the hotel and are not sure where they can park their car. How do they ask?

Where does the porter advise them to park?

Put it all together

1   Match the English with the Portuguese phrases.

a   **Tem . . . ?**   I've booked . . .
b   **Reservei . . .**   Can I . . . ?
c   **Queria . . .**   Do you have . . . ?
d   **Posso . . .**   I'd like . . .

2   You want to stay at Hotel Bela Vista and you write a letter to the manager to book a room. Fill in the blanks.

Lisboa, 13 de Agosto de 2003
Sr Gerente,
Queria reservar (a) .... (b) ...., (c) ...., de
(d) .... a (e) ...., em nome de (f) ....

a   a double room   b   with bath
c   for three nights   d   23rd September
e   25th September   f   your name

> **o gerente** manager
> **reservar** to book

3   If you asked the manager of this hotel the following questions would he answer **Sim** or **Não**?

Hotel Dom Henrique ★★★
Portimão – Algarve
- perto da praia
- 32 quartos com banho, TV, vista para o mar
- fechado 30 de Novembro – 1 Março

		Sim	Não
a	**Há um restaurante no hotel?**		
b	**Tem piscina?**		
c	**O hotel é longe da praia?**		
d	**Está aberto em Março?**		

Now you're talking!

I Imagine you are Mr Brett and you have gone to a hotel to ask for a room. The receptionist greets you.

◇ **Bom dia. Faz favor.**
◆ Ask if she has a room.
◇ **Para uma pessoa?**
◆ Say yes; say it's for three nights.
◇ **Sim, há um quarto no terceiro piso.**
◆ Ask how much it is.
◇ **€50 por noite. O seu nome?**
◆ Say your name is Lionel Brett.
◇ **Como se escreve Brett?**
◆ Spell BRETT.

2 Now imagine you are Mrs Bustamante and you telephone the hotel to book a room.

◆ Say hello.
◇ **Hotel Central. Boa tarde.**
◆ Greet the person and ask if they have a room for a week.
◇ **Simples ou de casal?**
◆ Say a double room.
◇ **O seu nome?**
◆ Say your name is Maria Bustamante.
◇ **Como se escreve Bustamante?**
◆ Spell BUSTAMANTE.

3 You arrive at a hotel where you have booked a room. You need to:

◆ say you've booked a room for two nights
◆ give your name and spell it
◆ specify with bath
◆ ask if you can park near the hotel

1   How do you say 'hello' on the phone?
2   How would you say 'for the 21st April'?
3   What is a **chave**?
4   What would a notice saying **Não estacionar** mean?
5   Which month follows **Junho**?
6   When would you use **posso** and when **podemos**?
7   What does **rés-do-chão** mean?
8   What is **um quarto com duas camas**?
9   Which of these means '3rd May': **treze**, **três**, **trinta de Maio**

Now check whether you can . . .

■   say you've booked a room

■   ask whether a room is available

■   ask for a room and specify single or double

■   say whether you want a room with or without a bath or shower

■   say how long you want the room for

■   understand and specify dates

■   spell your name in Portuguese

If you travel to Portugal with someone else, you may sometimes want to be able to say 'we' instead of 'I'. For many verbs (the **-ar** group) this involves substituting the **-o** ending with **-amos**:

moro	I live	**moramos**	we live
trabalho	I work	**trabalhamos**	we work

The other groups of verbs (**-er** and **-ir**) have different patterns of endings, and there are also some exceptions:

sou	I am	**somos**	we are

For more information see Grammar on page 120.

9 NOVE

A que horas parte?

- asking if there is a bus or coach
- checking train times
- buying tickets
- checking travel details

Em Portugal . . .

if you travel by public transport you'll find that the fares are quite reasonable and that **autocarros** (buses), **comboios** (trains) and **camionetas** (coaches) are frequent and generally reliable. In Lisbon and Oporto there are still **eléctricos** (trams) and in some parts of the city **elevadores** (cable cars) that take you up and down the high hills. In Lisbon there is also a **metro** (underground). **Camionetas** (coaches) will usually take you to the main cities and if you want to travel by **avião** (plane) there are international **aeroportos** (airports) at Lisbon, Oporto, Faro, Madeira and the Azores.

Asking if there is a bus or coach . . .

1   Listen to these key phrases.

Há um autocarro para . . . ?	Is there a bus to . . . ?
Há uma camioneta para . . . ?	Is there a coach to . . . ?
Há, sim	Yes, there is
Não há não	No, there isn't
Quando parte?	When does it leave?
Há um/uma . . .	There is one . . .
. . . às dez horas	. . . at 10 o'clock

Em português . . .

to say the time at which something takes place you use **à** or **às** + number. The word **hora/s** (hour/s) is sometimes added.

à	**à uma (hora)**	at 1 o'clock
às	**às duas (horas)**	at 2 o'clock
	às nove (horas)	at 9 o'clock

To say the time of day you use these expressions:

da manhã	in the morning
da tarde	in the afternoon

2   Carlos asks at the tourist office about the availability of coaches and buses. Listen and note down the departure times.

Vilamoura	....	Lagos	....
Braga	....	O aeroporto	....

3   At the coach station Maria asks about departure times. How does she ask if there is a coach to Viana do Castelo?

How does she ask when the coach to Faro leaves?

4   How would you ask if there is:

- a coach to Oporto?
- a bus to the station?

. . . and checking train times

5 Listen to these key phrases.

A que horas . . .	At what time . . .
parte o próximo comboio	does the next train leave
. . . para Braga?	. . . for Braga?
A que horas . . .	At what time . . .
chega o comboio	does the train arrive
. . . a Braga?	. . . in Braga?
. . . de Braga?	. . . from Braga?

Em português . . .

train times are usually given in the 24 hour clock. Hours are separated from minutes by **e** (and).

à uma e trinta	at 01.30
às nove e vinte	at 09.20
às catorze e cinquenta e dois	at 14.52

6 Steve asks about the **partidas** (departures) and **chegadas** (arrivals) of trains to various cities. He writes down the times but forgets to write down the cities. As you listen, can you match them up correctly?

partida	chegada	cidade
07.35	09.40	....
09.30	....	
10.00	....	
07.45	10.15	....

Viseu
Faro
Braga
Lagos

7 Now can you ask:

- what time the next train to Faro leaves?
- what time the train arrives in Faro?
- what time the train from Lisbon arrives?

Buying tickets . . .

1   Listen to these key phrases.

Um bilhete para . . .	A ticket to . . .
Só de ida . . .	Single . . .
. . . ou de ida e volta?	. . . or return?
(de) primeira classe	first class
(de) segunda classe	second class
para o intercidades	for the intercity
De que linha parte?	Which platform does it leave from?

2   Pedro de Sousa is an employee (**empregado**) at the train station in Lisbon. Listen and record the details of five tickets he sells.

destino	ida e volta / só ida	classe	para o intercidades / sim/não
Faro			
Braga			
Coimbra			
Lagos			
Oporto			

3   Listen again, and this time decide:

    a   Which platforms do these trains leave from?

        Braga ....   Oporto ....   Faro ....

    b   What time does the train to Coimbra leave?   ....

    c   When does it arrive in Coimbra?   ....

4   How would you ask for the following?

- a return ticket to Lagos
- a first class single ticket to Coimbra
- a return ticket for the intercity to Oporto

. . . and checking travel details

5 Listen to these key phrases.

É directo?	Is it a through train?
Não é não	No, it's not
Tenho de . . . ?	Do I have to . . . ?
Tem de . . .	You have to . . .
. . . mudar	. . . change
. . . reservar lugar	. . . make a seat reservation
hoje/amanhã	today/tomorrow
Não compreendo	I don't understand

6 Listen to Marta asking for information about travelling by train on **um feriado** (bank holiday). Fill in the gaps in the conversation.

Marta	**Há comboio para Braga amanhã, feriado?**
Empregado	**Há sim.**
Marta	**É directo?**
Empregado	**Não é não. A senhora .... mudar no Porto.**
Marta	**................. reservar lugar?**
Empregado	**Sim e .... reservar hoje.**

7 At the **Informações** (information desk) two people check the details of their journey. Listen to the recording several times and decide if each statement is **verdadeiro** or **falso**. The first one has been done for you.

		V	F
a	The man wants to go to Viana do Castelo.	✓	
b	He has to change trains.		
c	He doesn't need to reserve a seat.		
d	His train leaves from platform 5.		
e	The woman wants to travel by coach.		
f	The coach arrives at 11.15.		
g	She buys a return ticket.		

Put it all together

1 Fill in the blanks, using the words in the box:

   a   **Quanto custa um bilhete de ida e ....?**

   b   **................ mudar no Porto?**

   c   **Há um comboio .... Évora?**

   d   **A camioneta para Faro .... de Lisboa .... da manhã.**

   e   **................ um eléctrico para o Mosteiro dos Jerónimos?**

   f   **A que .... chega o avião de Londres? – .... às onze horas.**

> para
> há
> horas
> parte
> tenho de
> às nove
> volta
> chega

2 How would you say the following times in Portuguese?

   a   at 1 o'clock   *b*   at 07.25

   c   at 10 o'clock   *d*   at 13.00

   e   at 16.15   *f*   at 22.30

3 Can you match the questions to the answers?

   a   **Sim, há uma às 11 horas.**

   b   **O comboio de Lisboa chega à uma hora.**

   c   **Um bilhete só de ida.**

   d   **O comboio parte da linha dois.**

   e   **Sim, tem de reservar lugar.**

   f   **Não, tem de mudar.**

      1   **Tenho de reservar lugar?**

      2   **A que horas chega o comboio de Lisboa?**

      3   **O comboio é directo?**

      4   **Há uma camioneta para Lagos?**

      5   **Só de ida ou de ida e volta?**

      6   **De que linha parte o comboio para Faro?**

"Now you're talking!

1   Imagine you're at the ticket office in the station at Oporto. First, you
    want to go by train to Braga.

    ◆ Tell the ticket clerk that you want a ticket to Braga.
    ◇ **Só de ida ou de ida e volta?**
    ◆ Say you want a single ticket, then ask how much it is.
    ◇ **De primeira ou segunda classe?**
    ◆ Say first class.
    ◇ **Primeira classe para Braga . . . €10,50.**
    ◆ Ask at what time it leaves.
    ◇ **O comboio parte às três horas.**
    ◆ Ask from which platform.
    ◇ **Da linha dois.**

2   Next, you go to the coach station to ask for information about
    coaches from Coimbra to Viana do Castelo.

    ◇ **Diga.**
    ◆ Ask if there's a coach to Viana do Castelo.
    ◇ **Sim, há uma de meia em meia hora.**
    ◆ Ask if you have to book.
    ◇ **Não, não tem de reservar lugar.**
    ◆ Ask how much the ticket costs.
    ◇ **€9.**
    ◆ Ask what time the coach arrives in Viana do Castelo.
    ◇ **Chega a Viana do Castelo às 11.45.**
    ◆ Say you'd like a return ticket.

3   Two days later you decide to travel to Coimbra by train. For this
    activity you need to be able to:

    ◆ ask if there is a direct train to Coimbra
    ◆ ask where you have to change
    ◆ ask how much a return ticket costs
    ◆ say you want a ticket

Quiz

1   Which is the odd one out?
    bilhete   **comboio**   **camioneta**   **autocarro**

2   If you heard someone say **Há um autocarro para a estação?** what would they be asking?

3   Do **Chegadas** refer to Arrivals or Departures?

4   If you want a ticket to Lisbon do you say **Um bilhete para Lisboa** or **Um bilhete de Lisboa**?

5   How would you say to someone: 'It leaves at 5.30'?

6   What does **Não compreendo** mean?

7   If you want to ask 'Do I have to change?' would you use **tem de** or **tenho de**?

8   Does **amanhã** mean 'tomorrow' or 'in the morning'?

9   When would you meet a train if you were told **chega às vinte e duas e quarenta e nove**?

Now check whether you can . . .

■   ask if there's a bus or a coach going to a particular place

■   ask when or at what time trains (or other means of transport) depart and arrive

■   find out from which platform a train leaves

■   find out whether you have to make a seat reservation

■   ask for a single or return ticket

■   ask if you have to change

If you feel a bit overwhelmed by the amount of vocabulary and phrases you've met, go back to one of the early units to prove to yourself that you know a lot more than you think. Also try and improve on what you've learnt by identifying any strengths and weaknesses. The more you practise and build on your strengths, the easier it will be to find new ways of dealing with the weaknesses.

10
DEZ

Bom apetite!

- reading the menu
- asking about items on the menu
- ordering a meal
- saying what you like and don't like
- paying compliments

Em Portugal . . .

meals tend to be nourishing and substantial and consist of several courses: **entradas** (starters) or **sopas** (soups), **carnes** (meat dishes) or **peixes** (fish dishes) with **acompanhamentos** (side orders) and a **sobremesa** (dessert). In some restaurants you can order **meia dose** (half a portion) of a dish. Many restaurants will offer a **prato do dia** (dish of the day) which is a reasonably-priced meal in itself. When ordering wine you can ask for **meia garrafa** (half a bottle) or **uma garrafa** (a bottle).

At the start of a meal you usually wish people **Bom apetite!** (Enjoy your meal!)

EMENTA

Entradas

Camarões ou Gambas
Ameijoas à Trindade
Melão com presunto
Paté de pato com pão torrado

Starters, often consisting of shellfish such as **camarões** (shrimps), cold meats, etc. or soup such as **caldo verde** (green cabbage soup)

Sopas

Sopa do dia
Caldo verde

Fish course which might include **arroz de marisco** (seafood risotto), **lulas** (squid), the traditional **bacalhau** (salted cod) or **carapaus** (jack-fish)

Peixes

Arroz de marisco
Sardinhas grelhadas
Bacalhau à Zé do Pipo
Lulas fritas
Carapaus com molho à Espanhola

Carnes

Bife à casa
Espetada de carne
Febras grelhadas
Frango no churrasco
Carne de porco à Alentejana

Meat and poultry, often served with a side dish of salad or vegetables such as **cenouras** (carrots), **espinafres** (spinach) or **feijão verde** (haricot beans)

Acompanhamentos

Salada de tomate ou Salada mista
Espinafres, cenouras ou feijão verde
Batatas fritas, cozidas ou puré de batata
Arroz

Sobremesa

Baba de Camelo
Pudim flan
Bolo de chocolate
Arroz doce
Fruta da época

Desserts might include **pudim flan** (crème caramel), **Baba de Camelo** (mousse made with condensed milk), **gelado** (ice cream) and **arroz doce** (rice pudding). **Bolo** is a cake.

Reading the menu

I Read the following notes and then try to work out the meanings of the dishes on the menu. Use the glossary where necessary.

Here are some general terms referring to dishes . . .

. . . do dia	. . . of the day
. . . da época	. . . in season
. . . mista	mixed . . .
. . . da casa	house . . .

. . . and some methods or the style in which they are cooked:

frito	fried	**no churrasco**	barbecued
grelhado	grilled	**à Espanhola**	Spanish style
assado	roast, baked	**à casa**	house style
cozido	boiled	**com molho**	with sauce
torrado	toasted		

Fresh fish and seafood is plentiful: **lulas** (squid), **camarões** (shrimps), **gambas** (prawns), **sardinhas** (sardines), **pescada** (hake), **carapaus** (jack-fish) and **bacalhau** (salted cod) are commonly found. **Ameijoas** are clams.

Meat can be **vaca** (beef), **porco** (pork), **borrego** (lamb), or perhaps **leitão** (sucking-pig) or **cabrito** (kid). **Presunto** is smoked ham. Poultry includes **frango** or **galinha** (chicken), **perú** (turkey) and **pato** (duck).

Bife is a steak, **espetada** a kebab, **febras** are fillets (usually pork), and **costeletas** chops.

Famous dishes include the following:

cozido à Portuguesa (meat and vegetable stew)
carne de porco à Alentejana (pork with clams)

Asking about items on the menu

1 Listen to these key phrases.

Uma mesa para três pessoas A table for three
O que é . . . ? What is . . . ?
Como é? What's it like?
Como são? What are they like?

2 Carlos, Maria and Steve are shown to a table in the Restaurante do Mar. Listen as they ask about some of the items on the menu (p. 88) and tick the ones you hear.

3 Listen to more of their conversation. How does Steve ask what the **prato do dia** is? What does it consist of?

Lulas grelhadas   **Espetada de lulas**   **Febras grelhadas**

4 Listen as the waitress describes **bacalhau à Zé do Pipo**. Can you work out what it is and how it's cooked?

Is it . . .	fish	meat?
Is it . . .	boiled	baked?
Does it come with . . .	chips	mashed potatoes?
	vegetables	salad?

5 Carlos wants to know the ingredients of **carne de porco à Alentejana**. How does he ask?

Listen as the waitress lists the ingredients and tick them as you hear them. Can you fill in the missing ingredient?

....

CARNE DE PORCO À ALENTEJANA

porco
ameijoas (clams)
....
tomates

Ordering a meal

1 Listen to these key phrases

Estão prontos/as a pedir?	Are you ready to order?
O Senhor/A Senhora . . .	What are you going to have?
. . . o que vai comer?	
Que recomenda?	What do you recommend?
Eu vou comer . . .	I'm going to have (eat) . . .
Para mim . . .	For me . . .
Para beber?	To drink?

2 The waitress comes over to ask if Carlos, Maria and Steve are now ready to order. What do they each order as starters?

Carlos .... Maria .... Steve ....

3 Listen as they order their main dishes and complete the conversation.

Empregada **O Senhor, o que .... comer?**
Steve **Vou comer o prato ....**
Maria **Para .... as febras grelhadas.**
Carlos **................ recomenda?**

4 The waitress asks them what they want to drink. What do they order? Underline the drinks and tick the quantities.

	garrafa	meia garrafa	copo
água sem gás/com gás	▨	▨	▨
sumo de laranja	▨	▨	▨
cerveja	▨	▨	▨
vinho branco/tinto	▨	▨	▨

5 How would you say you'll have the following?

● the soup of the day   ● a mixed salad   ● the grilled sardines

Saying what you like and don't like

1 Listen to these key phrases.

O que tem de sobremesa?	What do you have for dessert?
(Eu) gosto de . . .	I like . . .
(Eu) não gosto de . . .	I don't like . . .
Gosta de . . . ?	Do you like . . . ? (**você**)
Gostas de . . . ?	Do you like . . . ? (**tu**)
Também gosto	I like it too
Gosto muito	I like it very much

2 Steve, Carlos and Maria are now ready for a **sobremesa**. How do they ask what there is? Listen as the waitress answers, and tick the desserts you hear.

> ### Sobremesas
> ....
>
> arroz doce
>
> mousse de chocolate
>
> bolo de chocolate
>
> gelados
>
> bolo de mel
>
> pudim flan
>
> tarte de maçã
>
> Baba de Camelo
>
> fruta da época

Em português . . .

when replying to a question, you usually include the verb in the reply, e.g.

Gosta de arroz doce?   **Sim, gosto**   Yes, I do
Gosta das gambas?   **Não, não gosto**   No, I don't

'I like it' and 'I like them' are both **gosto**.

3 Listen as Carlos, Maria and Steve discuss which desserts they like.

How does Carlos say he doesn't like **pudim flan**?
How does Steve say he likes **arroz doce**?
Do they all like **Baba de Camelo**?

4 How would you say you like/don't like rice pudding?

Paying compliments

1 Listen to these key phrases.

Está tudo bem?	Is everything all right?
Sim, está	Yes it is
É . . .	It's . . .
. . . bom (m.), **boa** (f.)	. . . good
São . . .	They're . . .
. . . bons (m.), **boas** (f.)	. . . good
óptimo/a, muito doce	excellent, very sweet

2 The waiter asks four customers **Está tudo bem?** Listen and tick any comments which you hear.

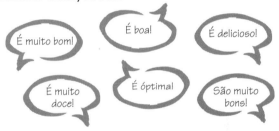

Em português . . .

to form the plural of words ending in **-m**, you omit the **-m** and add **-ns**:

Os carapaus são bons
Os bolos são muito bons

muito (very) does not change.

3 At Maria, Steve and Carlos's table the waitress asks them if everything is all right. What does Carlos say about the **Baba de Camelo**?
What does Maria say about the **pudim flan**?
What does Steve think of the **arroz doce**?

4 How would you say the soup is very good?

Put it all together

1 Complete the phrases on the left with the correct comments on the right.

a **A carne . . .**   **são muito boas**
b **As sardinhas . . .**   **é óptima**
c **O bolo . . .**   **são bons**
d **Os bifes . . .**   **é delicioso**

2 Which of the following are starters and which are main dishes?

Caldo verde, frango no churrasco, bacalhau cozido, melão com presunto, lulas fritas, paté de pato

Entradas e sopas	Peixes e carnes
....	....
....	....
....	....

3 Which answer fits each question?

a **Gostas de vinho branco?**   **Hoje o bife é bom.**
b **O Senhor o que vai comer?** **Sim, está.**
c **Está tudo bem?**   **Sim, gosto.**
d **Que recomenda?**   **A carne de porco, por favor.**

4 Below is a conversation in a restaurant between the waiter and a couple. Put the sentences in order.

a **Uma garrafa de vinho da casa.**
b **Sim, eu vou comer o bacalhau cozido.**
c **Estão prontos a pedir?**
d **A espetada de lulas, por favor.**
e **E para beber?**
f **E a senhora o que vai comer?**

"Now you're talking!

1   Imagine you're going out for a meal at Cervejaria Portugália. The
waiter greets you.

◇ **Uma mesa para uma pessoa?**
◆ Say yes.
◇ **Está pronto a pedir?**
◆ Say you'd like the prawns, then the barbecued chicken with a
tomato salad.
◇ **Para beber?**
◆ Say you'd like a bottle of the house wine.
◇ **Branco ou tinto?**
◆ Say the red.

2   Later the waiter comes to your table to check that all is well.

◇ **Está tudo bem?**
◆ Say yes it is, the wine is excellent and the chicken is delicious.
◇ **Deseja sobremesa?**
◆ Say you'll have the cream caramel.
◇ **Café?**
◆ Say no.

3   You go to a restaurant with a work colleague who doesn't speak
much Portuguese.

◇ **Estão prontos a pedir?**
◆ Ask him what he recommends.
◇ **A carne de porco à Alentejana é muito boa.**
◆ Order the pork and clams for yourself and a house steak for your
friend.
◇ **E para beber?**
◆ Order two beers.

Quiz

1 What does **Que recomenda?** mean?
2 Would you use **Gosto** or **Gosta** to say you like something?
3 What is **meia dose de arroz de marisco**?
4 How would you say 'I'll have the cod'?
5 Which one of these is not a dessert?
   salada de fruta, puré de batata, tarte, arroz doce
6 How would you say 'The prawns are good'.
7 If someone asks you **O que vai comer?** are they referring to food or drink?
8 How would you say 'I don't like meat'.

Now check whether you can . . .

■ understand the main points of a Portuguese menu

■ ask about items on the menu

■ order a meal with drinks

■ say what you like and what you don't like

■ ask others what they like

■ pay a compliment

Congratulations! You have reached the end of *Talk Portuguese*.

Now prepare yourself for the **Ponto de controle 3** with some revision. Listen to the conversations again – the more you listen the more confident you will become. You can test your knowledge of the key phrases by covering up the English in the lists. Look back at the quizzes and checklists to assess how much you remember, and take every opportunity to speak Portuguese. Hold a conversation with yourself if there's nobody else available!

Ponto de controle 3

Imagine you've just arrived in Faro on a Saturday evening at the start of a holiday in Portugal.

I You make your way to Hotel Dom Henrique, where you've booked a room with a shower until Monday. After giving your name to the receptionist, which of the following would you say?

a **Tem um quarto simples com banho para duas noites?**
b **Reservei um quarto de casal com duche para três noites.**
c **Reservei um quarto simples com duche para duas noites.**

2 Listen to the receptionist's reply. Make a note in English of the two questions she asks you, and also of your room number and which floor your room is on.

a ....

b ....

c **Quarto** ....   **Piso** ....

3 You need some information. Ask the receptionist:

a if you can make a phone call
b if there is a tobacconist's nearby
c if the tourist office is open on Sunday
d if there is a coach to Évora

4 Here are her replies. Which answer fits each question from activity 3?

1 **Sim, a cinco minutos a pé.**
2 **Sim, o telefone é aqui à direita.**
3 **Há sim.**
4 **Sim. Está aberto todos os dias.**

5 You want to phone Pedro, a Portuguese friend whom you met on your last visit to Portugal. His phone number has changed, so you ring directory enquiries. As you listen to the operator, write his number down.

telefone: ....

6 The receptionist suggests some places you might like to visit in Évora. Which ones? Listen and tick the ones you hear.

The Maritime Museum ▪ The Modern Art Museum ▪
The castle ▪ The old part of the city ▪
The Temple of Diana ▪ The monastery ▪

7 On Sunday you decide to visit Évora, and you go to the coach station to buy a return ticket.

How do you ask the following?
a when the next coach leaves for Évora
b how much a return ticket costs

Now listen to the audio and make a note of the time the coach leaves and when it gets to Évora. Write down the price of the ticket.

Partida	Chegada	Preço
....	....	....

c Is the journey direct?

8 When you arrive at the coach station in Évora it's lunchtime and you're feeling hungry. How would you ask a passer-by whether there are any restaurants in the area? ....

Now listen to her reply and write down her instructions:

....

....

9 Once seated in the restaurant you scan the menu.

You decide you'd like the soup followed by grilled sardines and a mixed salad.

a What do you say?

To drink you'd like half a bottle of white wine and some mineral water.

b How do you order it?

Later the waitress comes back to ask if you want a dessert. You've already decided on the chocolate cake!

c How do you order your dessert?

> **Sopas e entradas**
> melão com presunto
> sopa do dia
> ....
>
> **Peixes e carnes**
> lulas fritas
> sardinhas grelhadas
> frango no churrasco
> ....
>
> **Sobremesa**
> tarte de maçã
> bolo de chocolate

10

You meet Pedro in a bar. Order a beer for yourself and a glass of red wine for Pedro, then ask how much it is.

a ....
Aqui tem.
b ....
€ 1,45.

Pedro tells you about his new girlfriend, Elisa. Can you work out what questions to ask about her, if these are his answers?

c ....
Ela é de Lisboa.

advogado/a lawyer

d ....
É advogada.
e ....
Tem 25 anos.

When Elisa comes to join you at the bar she wants to find out about you. Listen to the audio and answer her questions.

11 You're hoping to meet up with Pedro, but this might be difficult as he travels a lot for his company. Listen as he tells you what his plans are for next week and write them down in your diary.

Monday	Thursday
Tuesday	Friday
Wednesday	Saturday
	Sunday

12 Pedro shows you a leaflet about the hotel where he suggests you all meet up next weekend. Read the leaflet then answer the questions.

Pousada Dona Maria ★★★★

- Com jardim, piscina e restaurante.
- Vista panorâmica.
- Perto da praia. A vila é a cinco minutos a pé.
- Todos os quartos têm casa de banho privativa.

Preços

Quarto individual   € 50 por quarto por noite
Quarto de casal   € 70 por quarto por noite
O pequeno almoço está incluído.

a How far is it from the village ?
b What facilities does it have?
c Is the beach far?
d Are the prices per person or per room?
e Is breakfast included?
f What kind of hotel is it?

a vila village

Audio scripts and answers

This section contains scripts of all the conversations. Answers which consist of words and phrases from the conversations are given in bold type in the scripts. Other answers are given separately.

Unit I Bom dia!

Pages 8 & 9 Saying hello and goodbye

2 • **Bom dia**, Senhora Barbara.
   • **Boa tarde**, Senhor António.

3 • Boa noite, Dona Paula. **Como está?**
   • Bem **obrigada**, e **você?**

5 • **Adeus bom dia, Dona Paula.**
   • **Boa tarde. Até logo!**
   • **Tchau. Boa noite.**

6 08.00: Adeus, bom dia.
   14.00: Boa tarde, Senhora Fernanda.
   23.00: Boa noite, Senhor Luís.

7 • Boa tarde, Senhor Pedro. Como está?
   • Bom dia, Ana. Como estás?
   • Boa noite, Senhora Paula. Como está?

8 • Boa tarde, Senhor Pedro!
   • Boa noite, Senhora Paula!

Pages 10 & 11 Introducing yourself and getting to know people

2 • Boa noite. Eu sou **o João, João Reis**.

3 • A Senhora é?
   • **Sou** a Ana da Costa Passos.
   • Ah, Dona Ana. Como está?

4 • Olá, **eu sou o Fernando.** Tu és?
   • **Eu sou a Sandra.** Tudo bem?

6 • **Chamo-me** Luís de Castro. E você?
   Como se chama?

• **Chamo-me** Vanda Abreu. **Muito prazer.**
• **Muito prazer.**

7 • Olá! Chamo-me Carla Correia.
   • **Desculpe?**
   • Chamo-me Carla, Carla Correia.
   • Muito prazer.

8 • Olá! Como te chamas?
   • **Chamo-me Maria.**

Page 12 Put it all together

1 a Como está? b Muito prazer;
   c Bom dia! d Sou; e Boa noite; f Adeus;
   g Como se chama?

   a ESTÁ; b MUITO; c DIA; d SOU;
   e BOA; f ADEUS; g CHAMA

2 a Bom dia; b Boa tarde; c Olá! Tudo
   bem? d Adeus, boa noite!

Page 13 Now you're talking!

1 • Bom dia, a Senhora é?
   • **Sou a Carla Correia.**
   • Desculpe?
   • **Sou a Carla Correia.**
   • Ah! Sim, a Senhora Dona Carla Correia!

2 • Boa noite. Chamo-me Carlos Ribeiro.
   • **Muito prazer.**

3 • Boa tarde, Dona Carla, como está?
   • **Estou bem, obrigada. E o Senhor?**
   • Eu também estou bem, obrigado.
   • **Até logo.**

4 • Boa tarde. Chamo-me Paulo.
   • Eu chamo-me Ana.
   • **Eu chamo-me Carla. Como te chamas?**
   • Chamo-me Sandra.
   • **Adeus, boa tarde.**

Page 14 **Quiz**

1 Como te chamas? *2* Nice to meet you;
3 in the evening; *4* a man's name; *5* Bem,
obrigado/a; *6* tu; *7* Até logo; *8* ADEUS.

Unit 2 **Donde é?**

Pages 16 & 17 **Talking about your nationality and saying where you're from**

2 • Olá, como se chama?
  • Chamo-me **Carlo**.
  • Donde é?
  • **Sou italiano.**
  • E você, **Richard**?
  • Eu sou **inglês**, de Londres.
  • E você também é inglês?
  • Não, não sou inglês. Sou **irlandês**.
    Chamo-me Martin.
  Carlo is Italian; Richard is English; Martin is Irish.

3 • Eu sou **portuguesa**, sou de Lisboa.
    E você, Anna?
  • Eu sou de Cardiff. Eu sou **galesa**.
  • E você, Robert, donde é?
  • Sou **americano**. Sou de Chicago.
  Maria is Portuguese; Anna is Welsh; Robert is American.

4 galês – **galesa**; inglês – **inglesa**;
  escocês – **escocesa**; francês –
  francesa; americano – **americana**;
  brasileiro – **brasileira**; irlandês –
  irlandesa.

5 • Donde é, Véronique?
  • Sou **francesa**, de **Paris**.
  • E você, Tom?
  • **Sou inglês**, de **Manchester**.
  • E você, Katie, é **inglesa**?
  • Não, **não sou inglesa**, sou
    escocesa, de **Glasgow**.

6 • Andrew, é escocês?
  • Mary, é irlandesa?

• Sean, é americano?
• Carla, é italiana?
• Sim sou.
• Não, não sou irlandesa.
  Sou americana.

Page 18 **Saying what you do for a living**

2 • A Senhora como se chama?
  • Chamo-me Ana, Ana Fortes.
  • Eu chamo-me Pedro Correia.
    O que faz?
  • Sou artista. E o Senhor?
  • Sou estudante. E o Senhor?
  • Eu chamo-me Manuel de Oliveira.
    Sou dentista.
  Ana is an artist, Pedro a student and Manuel a dentist.

3 • Madalena, donde é?
  • Sou de Cascais.
  • O que faz?
  • Sou pintora.
  • E você, Fernando, donde é?
  • Sou de Braga e sou médico.
  • E você, João. Donde é? E o que faz?
  • Sou de Faro. Sou professor.
  Madalena: Cascais, painter; Fernando: Braga, doctor; João: Faro, teacher.

Page 19 **Giving your phone number**

3 • (1) Tem telefone?
  • Sim. É o três, um, três, dois, nove, dois.
  • (2) Tem telefone?
  • Sim. É o zero, dois, zero, sete, cinco, oito, dois, dois, quatro, cinco, seis.
  • (3) Tem telefone?
  • Sim. É o nove, sete, sete, três, seis, três, dois.
  • (4) Tem telefone?
  • Sim. É o oito, nove, um, cinco, quatro, seis, sete.
  1 = b; 2 = c; 3 = d; 4 = a

4 • O número é o oito, nove, zero, seis, zero, quatro.

- O número é o sete, sete, um, dois, sete, três.

Travel Agency: 89 06 04; Doctor's surgery: 77 12 73.

5 *a* sete, dois, três, quatro, quatro, cinco, cinco; *b* oito, nove, quatro, nove, oito, três, três; *c* zero, dois, zero, sete, cinco, seis, dois, um, quatro, três, dois; *d* zero, zero, quatro, quatro, dois, zero, oito, oito, nove, quatro, sete, um, seis, um.

Page 20 Put it all together

I INGLATERRA – ESPANHA – FRANÇA – ITÁLIA – BRASIL – ESCÓCIA – ALEMANHA – CANADÁ – IRLANDA

2 • Bom **dia**. Como **se** chama?
   • Chamo-me Martin. E **você**?
   • **Chamo-me** Anne. **Sou** francesa. Você **é** americano?
   • Não, sou inglês. Sou **de** Devon.
   • Eu sou de Paris. O que **faz**?
   • **Sou** jornalista.
   • Eu sou professora.

3 *a* Não, sou português; *b* Sou de Moçambique; *c* Sim, de Angola; *d* Sim, sou inglês; *e* Sim. É o 977 1221; *f* Sou artista.

Page 21 Now you're talking!

I • **Chamo-me + *your name*. Sou de + *your home town*. Donde é?**
   • Sou de Braga.
   • **O que faz?**
   • Sou pintor.
   • **Tem telefone?**
   • Sim. É o 275 6777.

2 • O Senhor Perry é inglês?
   • **Não, sou galês.**
   • Donde é?
   • **Sou de Glamorgan.**
   • O Senhor tem telefone?

- **Sim. É o zero, zero, quatro, quatro, três, três, nove, cinco, quatro, um, um.**

3 • **É italiana?**
   • Sim, sou. Sou de Roma.
   • **É artista?**
   • Não, não sou. Sou professora.

Page 22 Quiz

1 QUATRO; *2* Não sou inglês/inglesa; *3* Eu sou de Lisboa; *4* É brasileiro? *5* Não, não sou americano/a, sou irlandês/esa; *6* What you do for a living; *7* Tem telefone? *8* um, dois, três, quatro, cinco, seis; *9* Sou estudante.

Unit 3 Este é o Paulo

Page 24 Introducing someone

2 • Bom dia, Senhora Pereira. **Este** é o Senhor Luís Correia.
   • Muito prazer.
   • E **esta** é a Senhora Carla Fortuna.
   • Muito prazer.

3 • Esta é a Senhora **Advogada** Francisca Martins; Este é o Senhor **Doutor** Roberto Leal; Este é o Senhor **Engenheiro** Mário de Andrade; Esta é a Senhora **Doutora** Luisa Teixeira.
   Francisca is a lawyer; Roberto is a graduate; Mário is an engineer; Luisa is a graduate.

4 Este é o Senhor António Leal; Este é o Senhor Carlos Fortuna; Esta é a Dona Sofia Pereira; Este é o Senhor Engenheiro Fernando Correia.

Page 25 Talking about your family

2 • **É casada?**
   • Sim, sou.
   • **Tem filhos?**

- Sim, tenho. **Tenho um filho e uma filha.** E você?
- Eu não sou casado. Sou viúvo.
- Tem filhos?
- **Não, não tenho filhos.**

Doutor Ferreira has no children.

3
- Esta é **a minha** irmã Marta, este é **o meu** irmão Pedro e este é **o meu** pai José.

4
- Tens irmãos?
- **Não, não tenho.**

Page 26 Saying how old you are

2 trinta e sete; noventa e dois; sessenta e nove; setenta e oito
missing number: cinquenta e sete

4
- Cristina, **quantos anos tens?**
- **Tenho dezanove anos.**
- Eu tenho vinte anos. E tu, Sofia?
- Eu tenho dezoito.
Cristina is 19, Miguel is 20 and Sofia is 18.

5
- Quantos anos **tem?**
- **Tenho vinte e nove anos.**

Page 27 Talking about another person

1
- Tem filhos?
- Sim, tenho dois. Um filho e uma filha.
- Como se chama o seu filho?
- Daniel.
- Quantos anos tem?
- O Daniel tem cinco anos.
- Como se chama a sua filha?
- Teresa.
- Ela quantos anos tem?
- Sete.
a F (he's Daniel); b V; c V; d F (she's seven).

2
- Chamo-me Daniel. Esta é a minha esposa, Paula e esta é o meu filho. Ele tem 19 anos *(b)*
- Chamo-me Maria. Este é o meu filho

e esta é a minha filha. *(a)*.
- Chamo-me Alexandra. Sou casada e tenho uma filha. Este é o meu esposo, Carlos. *(c)*.

Page 28 Put it all together

1 *a* Luisa; *b* Manuel; *c* Carlos; *d* Pedro; *e* Ana.

2 59; 55; 23; 13; 15; 31; 39.

3
- Não, não tenho.
- Sim tenho. Tenho ..... filha(s) e ..... filho(s).
- Tenho ..... irmã(s) e ..... irmão(s).

Page 29 Now you're talking!

1
- É casado?
- **Sim, sou casado.**
- Tem filhos?
- **Tenho um filho. Chama-se David.**
- Quantos anos tem?
- **Ele tem vinte e seis anos.**
- É casado?
- **Sim, é casado.**
- Tem filhos?
- **Não, não tem filhos. É casada?**
- Sim, sou casada.
- **Tem filhos?**
- Eu tenho uma filha. Ela chama-se Ana.
- **Quantos anos tem?**
- Tem quinze anos.

2
- Como se chama ele?
- **Ele chama-se Pedro.**
- Quantos anos tem?
- **Tem vinte e nove anos.**
- É casado?
- **Não, não é casado. É solteiro.**

3
- Como se chama?
- **Chamo-me Isabel.**
- Quantos anos tem?
- **Tenho quarenta e cinco anos.**
- É casada?
- **Sim, sou casada.**
- Tem filhos?

- **Sim, tenho uma filha. Chama-se Rita.**

Page 30 **Quiz**

1 Quantos anos tens? *2* Esta é; *3* Este é o Doutor . . .; *4* Tenho . . . anos; *5* She; *6* If you have children − Sim, tenho. If you don't − Não, não tenho; *7* advogado; *8* quinze, vinte e cinco, quarenta.

Unit 4 **Um café, por favor**

Pages 32 & 33 **Ordering a drink in a bar**

2 • Faz favor?
   • **Uma bica**, por favor.

3 • Uma cerveja, por favor.
   • Uma limonada, faz favor.
   Natália − beer; Alberto − lemonade.

4 • Faz favor! Um batido de chocolate, por favor.
   • Um batido de morango.
   Paulo − chocolate flavour; João − strawberry flavour.

5 • Faz favor?
   • Um Martini.
   • Uhm . . . Como se diz em português 'wine'?
   • Vinho?
   • Ah sim, vinho. Vinho do Porto, faz favor.
   Wine − vinho.

6 • Obrigado.
   • **De nada.**

7 • Um vinho da casa, por favor.
   • Branco ou tinto?
   • Branco.
   • E para o Senhor?
   • Branco, por favor.
   Both want white wine.

8 Uma bica, um galão e um copo de vinho tinto, por favor.

Page 34 **Offering, accepting or refusing**

2 • Que deseja?
   • Um café com leite, por favor.
   • E o Senhor Pereira? Deseja um café?
   • Não, obrigado.
   • Uma cerveja?
   • Sim, por favor.
   No, he wants a beer.

3 • Que deseja, Carlos?
   • Um galão, faz favor.
   • Luisa?
   • Também um galão.
   • Para si, Fernando?
   • Uma cerveja, por favor.
   • Faz favor!
   • Dois **galões** e duas **cervejas**.
   dois − duas

Page 35 **Paying for your drinks**
(In informal spoken Portuguese, you will often hear prices without the 'e' after euros)

2 seis euros setenta e cinco; um euro cinquenta; cinco euros cinquenta.
   €6,75; €1,50; €5,50

3 • Quanto é?
   • Quatro euros oitenta e sete.
   • Quanto é?
   • Seis euros sessenta e cinco.
   €4,87; €6,65

Page 36 **Put it all together**

1 **Um** copo de vinho; **um** gelado; **um** leite de chocolate; **um** chá com leite; **uma** limonada; **um** batido de banana. **Dois** copos de vinho; **dois** gelados; **dois** leites de chocolate; **dois** chás com leite; **duas** limonadas; **dois** batidos de banana.

2 • Faz favor! Que deseja?
   • Uma cerveja.

- E para si?
- Um conhaque.
- Quanto é?
- € 2,25.

3 *a* cinquenta cêntimos; *b* um euro e quarenta; *c* um euro e quinze; *d* dois euros e vinte.

Page 37 Now you're talking!

1
- Faz favor!
- **Maria, que deseja?**
- Um galão, por favor.
- **Bernardo, e você, que deseja?**
- Uma bica, por favor.
- **Bom dia! Um galão e duas bicas, por favor.**
- **Quanto é?**
- Dois euros sessenta

2
- Deseja um café?
- **Sim, por favor. Uma meia de leite.**

3
- Que deseja?
- **Como se diz em português 'a black coffee'?**

4
- **Que desejam?**
- Um copo de vinho branco.
- Um copo de vinho tinto, por favor.
- **Faz favor! Dois copos de vinho, um branco e um tinto, e uma cerveja, por favor.**
- Obrigado/a.
- Tchim, tchim!

Page 38 Quiz

1 por favor, faz favor; *2* to order; *3* Como se diz em português 'vanilla'? *4* um sumo, uma cerveja, uma bica, um copo de vinho; *5* Tchim, tchim! *6* dois galões, duas águas, duas bicas; *7* Deseja um café? *8* cinco euros e oitenta, quatro euros e cinquenta e cinco, um euro e sessenta e sete, onze euros e noventa; *9* 'um garoto' is a small white coffee, 'uma meia de leite' is a large white coffee, 'um

galão' is a white coffee in a glass.

Ponto de controle 1 (Pages 39–42)

1
- Bom dia. Eu sou a Paula de Oliveira.
- Chamo-me Arlete Cardoso. Este é o meu filho Carlos.
- Olá, Carlos.
- Olá.
- És estudante, Carlos?
- Sim, sou.
- Quantos anos tens?
- Quinze.
- A Dona Arlete é de Lisboa?
- Não. Eu sou de Braga.
- O que faz?
- Sou pintora. O meu esposo é professor de português e francês.
a portuguesa; *b* Braga; *c* pintora (painter); *d* casada (married); *e* um filho (a son); *f* quinze (15).

2
- Olá!
- Olá! É inglesa?
- Não, não sou inglesa. Sou italiana. E você?
- Sou de Faro. Sou português.
- O que faz?
- Sou dentista.
- Eu sou recepcionista.
Rita – italiana, recepcionista; Carlos: – português, dentista.

3
- Faz favor?
- Uma cerveja, por favor.
- E para si?
- Uma bica.
Rita – uma cerveja (beer); Carlos – uma bica (small black coffee).

4
- Um copo de vinho tinto – oitenta e cinco cêntimos; um copo de leite – setenta cêntimos e um sumo de laranja natural – oitenta cêntimos.
red wine – € 0,85; glass of milk – € 0,70; orange juice – € 0,80

5 **bebidas**: bicas, limonadas, galões,

sumos de ananás;

profissões: professores, estudantes, escritores, jornalistas.

6 professora, estudante, escritora, jornalista.

7 *a* um garoto; *b* um conhaque; *c* uma água; *d* um batido.

8 *a* Chamo-me Renata. Sou alemã, de Hamburgo; *b* Tenho 15 anos; *c* Tenho dois irmãos, o Hanz de 17 anos e o Franz de 20 anos; *d* O meu pai é advogado; *e* A minha mãe é professora de inglês.

9 • Bom dia. Eu sou **o** Pierre Larousse.
   • Ilda Rosas. Muito prazer. **Esta** é a Teresa.
   • **Muito prazer.**
   • Eu **sou** de Lion em França. E você, **donde** é?
   • Eu sou de Madrid. A Teresa **é** de Valencia.

10 *a* baunilha; *b* solteiro; *c* alemão; *d* anos.

11 *a* É casado? *b* Tudo bem? *c* Para si? *d* Sou inglês; *e* O que faz?

12 *a* Como se chama? *b* Donde é? *c* Quantos anos tem? *d* O que faz? *e* Tem telefone?

13 *a* falso; *b* verdadeiro; *c* falso; *d* falso; *e* verdadeiro; *f* verdadeiro

Unit 5 **Desculpe, onde é a estação?**

Pages 44 & 45 **Asking where something is and asking for help with the answer**

2 • Onde é a catedral?
   • A catedral é aqui.

• Onde é o mosteiro?
• O mosteiro é na rua Augusta.
• Onde é o banco de Portugal?
• O banco é ali.
• Onde é a estação?
• A estação é no centro da cidade.
• É longe?
• Cinco minutos a pé.
• E o jardim botânico?
• O jardim botânico é perto.

a **a catedral**; *b* **o mosteiro**; *c* **o banco**; *d* **a estação**; *e* **o jardim botânico**

4 • Desculpe, **onde são** as lojas?
   • As lojas? A **quinhentos** metros daqui.
   • **Pode repetir, por favor?**
   • **A quinhentos metros daqui.** Dez minutos a pé.
   The shops are 500 metres away. Steve doesn't understand and asks the passer-by to repeat.

5 • Desculpe, onde é o banco?
   • É ali, entre o museu e o hospital.
   • **Pode falar mais devagar, por favor?**
   • Ali, entre **o museu** e **o hospital**.
   Steve doesn't understand and asks the passer-by to speak slowly.

6 • Faz favor, onde é o castelo? É longe?
   • Não. É a um quilómetro daqui. É quinze minutos a pé.
   It's 1 kilometre away; 15 minutes' walk.

7 Onde é o banco?
   Onde é a Rua Augusta?
   Onde são as ruínas?

Pages 46 & 47 **Talking about where you live and work**

2 • Onde mora, Maria?
   • Moro em Faro, no **centro** de Faro, **na rua** do Alecrim.
   • E você, Isabel?
   • Eu moro na Praia da Luz.

- Eu moro no **campo**, a trinta quilómetros de Lagos.
3 Moro em Dublin; Moro no centro da cidade; Moro na rua King

5 ● Maria, onde trabalhas?
- **Trabalho num banco** em Lisboa.
- E tu, Paulo?
- Eu trabalho no centro de Cascais, num escritório.
- E eu trabalho numa loja, em Lisboa. E tu, Carlos, onde trabalhas?
- Eu trabalho num banco, no centro de Coimbra.

Maria in a bank; Paulo in an office; Isabel in a shop. Carlos also works in a bank.

Page 48 **Put it all together**

1 *a* **o** centro, **a** rua, **a** praça;
b **o** escritório, **a** loja, **o** colégio;
c **o** castelo, **a** estação, **o** museu;
d **o** porto, **a** praia, **a** ilha.

2 *a* Pode **falar** devagar?; *b* Pode **repetir?**; *c* Onde **é** o centro? *d* Onde **mora** o Fernando? *e* Onde **são** os restaurantes? *f* Não **trabalho**; *g* **Trabalhas** numa loja?

3 *a* Onde é a praia? *b* Pode repetir, por favor? *c* Onde mora? *d* Onde trabalha?

4 *a* **em** Cascais; *b* **na** rua Augusta; *c* no centro de Lisboa; *d* num escritório

Page 49 **Now you're talking!**

1 ● Olá, bom dia.
- **Bom dia. Onde é a catedral?**
- A catedral é na rua de São Miguel.
- **Onde é a rua de São Miguel?**
- É aqui.
- **É longe?**
- Não. É a duzentos metros daqui.
- **Obrigado/a. Adeus.**

2 ● O Museu da Marinha.

- **Pode repetir, por favor?**
- O Museu da Marinha. É entre o mosteiro e o jardim botânico. Não é longe – a cinco minutos a pé.
- **Obrigado/a. . . . entre o mosteiro e o jardim botânico.**

3 ● Donde é?
- **Sou + o/a +** *your name and nationality,* **sou de +** *where you come from.*
- Onde mora?
- **Moro em/no/na +** *your home town.*
- O que faz?
- **Sou +** *what you do for a living.*
- Onde trabalha?
- **Trabalho num/numa +** *type of workplace.*

4 ● **Onde mora?**
- Moro no campo.
- **É longe?**
- Não é longe – a vinte quilómetros daqui.

Page 50 **Quiz**

1 Moro em Brighton e trabalho em Londres; *2* Onde é o centro da cidade? *3* He doesn't work; *4* no; *5* Onde mora? *6* Pode repetir, por favor? *7* Ele trabalha na Avenida da Liberdade.

Unit 6 **Há um banco aqui perto?**

Pages 52 & 53 **Finding out what there is in town and when it's open**

2 *a* supermarket; *b* library; *c* museum; *d* baker's; *e* post office; *f* swimming pool; *g* language school; *h* chemist's.

3 ● **A escola de línguas?** Há uma escola de línguas aqui na parte velha da cidade.
- É longe?
- Não. Quinze minutos a pé.

- Há **um museu** na cidade?
- Sim, há o Museu de Arte Antiga.
- Onde é?
- Aqui na parte velha da cidade. E aqui é **o teatro,** em frente do museu. Aqui, a cinco minutos do museu, há **um supermercado**.
- Há **uma piscina** na parte velha da cidade?
- Não, não há uma piscina na parte velha da cidade. (Há uma na parte nova)
a Sim; b Sim; c Sim; d Não.

4 Há uma farmácia? Há um correio?

6 • A piscina está aberta **todos os dias**.
   • E o museu?
   • O museu está fechado aos **sábados** e aos **domingos**.
   • Há um mercado todos os dias?
   • Não. Há um mercado às **quintas-feiras**.

7 *a* O banco está aberto todos os dias? O supermercado está aberto todos os dias?
   b A padaria está aberta todos os dias? O supermercado está fechado aos domingos?

Pages 54 & 55 **Making simple enquiries and understanding directions**

2 • Onde é a casa de banho?
   • **Alí ao fundo, à direita.**

3 • Desculpe, **há um telefone aqui perto**?
   • Peço desculpa. Não sei.
   The passer-by doesn't know.

4 • Desculpe, há um telefone aqui perto?
   • **Sempre em frente**, depois à **direita**.

5 • Há um banco aqui perto?
   • Na primeira rua à direita, depois sempre em frente. É à esquerda a duzentos metros do Hotel Central.
   First street on the right then straight ahead. It's

on the left, 200 metres from the Hotel Central.

7 • Desculpe. Onde é o castelo?
   • É na parte velha da cidade.
   • É longe?
   • É a trinta minutos a pé.
   • Onde é a paragem do autocarro?
   • É em frente da estação.
   The castle is in the old part of the city, a 30 minute walk. Opposite the station.

8 • Olha, Isabel, o teatro é ali.
   • Onde?
   • Ali, em frente do parque.
   • E o mosteiro? Onde é?
   • É ali à esquerda.
   • As lojas são ali no centro.
   • Onde é a piscina?
   • Em frente da praia.
   a falso (it's opposite the park);
   b verdadeiro; c verdadeiro.

Page 56 **Put it all together**

1 *a* Not on Sundays; *b* on Wednesdays; *c* on Mondays; *d* Yes.

2 *a* direita; *b* rua do Porto, direita; *c* em frente do; *d* ao fundo, esquerda.

Page 57 **Now you're talking!**

1 • Bom dia.
   • **Bom dia. Há um banco aqui perto?**
   • Sim, há um em frente do café.
   • **Há uma farmácia aqui perto?**
   • Sim, a farmácia é aqui em frente.
   • **Onde é a casa de banho?**
   • É aqui ao fundo à direita.

2 • **Há um Centro de Turismo na parte velha da cidade?**
   • Sim, há um na segunda rua à esquerda.
   • **Na segunda rua à esquerda. Obrigado/a.**

3 • Faz favor, uma planta da cidade.
   • **Obrigado/a. Onde é o museu?**
   • Na primeira rua à esquerda.

- **Na primeira rua à esquerda. Está aberto hoje?**
- Sim, está aberto todos os dias.
- **Onde é o castelo?**
- Aqui é o castelo e aqui é a paragem do autocarro número 43.
- **É antes do museu?**
- Não, a paragem é depois do museu.
- **O castelo está aberto às segundas-feiras?**
- Não o castelo está fechado às segundas-feiras.

Page 58 **Quiz**

1 Há um café aqui perto? *2* aberta;
3 Straight on, then the first on the left;
4 Tuesday; *5* Peço desculpa. Não sei;
6 rua; *7* Fridays; *8* Não trabalho aos domingos.

Unit 7 **Quanto custa?**

Page 60 **Asking and understanding the price**

2
- Bom dia. Diga.
- Quanto **custa** a revista?
- **Dois euros cinquenta.**
- E quanto **custa** o jornal?
- **Setenta e cinco cêntimos.**
- Os postais quanto **custam**?
- **Cinquenta cêntimos** cada.
- Faz favor.
- Uma revista, um jornal e três postais, quatro euros e setenta e cinco cêntimos.
magazine – € 2,50; newspaper – € 0,75; postcards – € 1,50; total – € 4,75.

3
- Diga.
- **Quanto custam os selos** para a União Européia?
- Cinquenta e cinco cêntimos.
- Três selos, por favor.
- Faz favor.
- Tem um cartão telefónico?
- Sim. De cinquenta impulsos ou de cem impulsos?
- De cinquenta impulsos. **Quanto custa?**
- Três euros.
- Quanto custa tudo?
- Três selos para a União Européia são um euro e sessenta e cinco, e o cartão quatro euros e sessenta e cinco.
Total cost – € 4,65

4 Quanto custam quatro selos? Quanto custa uma revista? Quanto custam dois postais?

Page 61 **Describing and commenting**

2
- Eu queria **um livro**.
- Há livros ali.
- Quanto custa este livro?
- Trinta e um euros e quarenta e três cêntimos.
- Ah, é demasiado caro!
- Olha, Isabel, **um saco de desporto**!
- É demasiado grande, Carlos. Eu queria **uma T-shirt**.
- Há T-shirts aqui.
- Uhm, esta é demasiado pequena.
- E esta?
- Esta sim, levo a T-shirt.

3
- *É demasiado grande – It's too big; Levo a T-shirt*

4
- A revista é cara. O livro é demasiado caro. A T-shirt é demasiado pequena. É demasiado grande!

Pages 62 & 63 **Buying food in a shop or market**

1
- um quilo de açúcar, meio quilo de queijo, trezentos gramas de fiambre, meio litro de azeite, uma garrafa de água mineral, uma garrafa de vinho tinto e dois pães de forma.
She forgets to write 'meio litro de azeite'.

3
- Dê-me **meio quilo** de café, por favor.
- Também queria **duas latas** de tomates.

4 ● Bom dia, senhora. Diga.
  ● Queria seis bananas e quatro pêssegos.
  ● Faz favor. Mais alguma coisa?
  ● Sim. Dê-me meio quilo de morangos. Ah, e um quilo de maçãs. Quanto custa tudo?
  ● Quatro euros setenta e três.
  Bananas, peaches, strawberries and apples.
5 ● Senhora, diga.
  ● Quatro quilos de batatas, por favor.
  ● É só?
  ● Dê-me dois quilos de cebolas e um quilo de tomates.
  ● Mais alguma coisa?
  ● Não. É só.
  batatas – quatro quilos; cebolas – dois quilos; tomates – um quilo.

6 ● Quanto custa o **bacalhau**?
  ● Dez euros o quilo.
  ● Ah, é demasiado caro! **Dê-me oito sardinhas,** faz favor.
  She asks about the cod but buys sardines which are cheaper.

7 *a* Quanto custa o jornal? Quanto custa a garrafa de vinho? Quanto custam os morangos?
  b Meio quilo de fiambre; duzentos e cinquenta gramas de queijo; uma lata de tomates.

Page 64 **Put it all together**

1 *a* Do you have? *b* That's all; *c* It's too expensive; *d* Give me; *e* How much is it? *f* Anything else? *g* How much are they?

2 **Banca da fruta**: maçãs, morangos, pêssegos;
  Banca do peixe: sardinhas, bacalhau, peixe espada;
  Tabacaria: selos, postais, jornal;
  Supermercado: queijo, fiambre, açúcar.

3 um quilo de batatas, quatrocentos gramas de fiambre, três quilos de

cebolas, meio quilo de queijo, uma garrafa de vinho branco.
4 *a* € 0,59; *b* € 9,47; *c* € 1,78; *d* Onze euros e oitenta e quatro cêntimos (€ 11,84).

Page 65 **Now you're talking!**

1 ● Bom dia. Diga.
  ● **Doze garrafas de vinho branco e seis garrafas de vinho tinto, por favor.**
  ● Mais alguma coisa?
  ● **Três garrafas de água mineral.**
  ● É só?
  ● **Doze garrafas de cerveja.**
  ● Cerveja Sagres?
  ● **Sim. Quanto é tudo?**

2 ● **Tem fiambre?**
  ● Sim, quanto?
  ● **Trezentos gramas.**
  ● Aqui está. Mais alguma coisa?
  ● **Meio quilo de queijo.**
  ● É só?
  ● **É só. Quanto é tudo?**

3 ● **Quanto custa um selo para a América?**
  ● Setenta cêntimos.
  ● **Três selos e três postais.**
  ● Três postais . . .
  ● **Quanto é tudo?**
  ● Três euros e dez.

Page 66 **Quiz**

1 Quanto custam as bananas? Quanto custa o gelado? Quanto custam os selos? Quanto custa o jornal? *2* Quanto custa um selo? *3* É demasiado cara; *4* a kilo of peaches; *5* vegetables; *6* fish; *7* Queria três garrafas de água mineral; *8* demasiado.

Ponto de controle 2 (Pages 67–70)

1 ● Desculpe, senhora. Onde é o clube de desporto?
  ● É no centro da cidade.
  ● É longe?

- Dez minutos a pé. É sempre em frente
  depois na segunda rua à esquerda.
- Obrigado.

*a in the city centre; b 10 minute walk;
c straight on then the second street on
the left.*

2 - No clube há uma sauna, um ginásio,
   um café e uma loja. Perto do clube há
   um campo de ténis.
   - Há uma piscina aqui perto?
   - Não, não há. A piscina é nos
   arredores da cidade. É a meia hora
   de autocarro. O clube está aberto
   todos os dias. Aos domingos está
   aberto só de manhã.
   *a sauna, gym, café, shop, tennis court.
   b open every day; Sundays mornings only*

3 - Quanto pesa?
   - Peso setenta e três quilos. E você?
   - Sessenta e dois e meio. E tenho um
   metro e cinquenta e cinco de altura.
   - Eu tenho um metro e setenta de
   altura.
   - Uhm . . . quantos anos tem? Vinte e
   sete?
   - Sim. Você também tem vinte e sete
   anos?
   - Sim. Uhm . . . morada – Rua
   Almirante Reis, número vinte e três.
   Telefone – oito, dois, dois, um, nove,
   cinco, quatro.
   *Tel: 822 1954; address: Rua Almirante
   Reis, 23; age: 27; height: 1m 55cm;
   weight: 62.5 kilos.*

4 - Bom dia. Diga.
   - Tem um fato de treino?
   - Sim. Faz favor.
   - É bonito, Maria. Quanto custa?
   - Cinquenta e três euros.
   - É muito caro! E as T-shirts?
   - Quinze euros cada.
   - Levo uma T-shirt. E tem calções . . .
   tamanho médio?
   - Sim. Faz favor.
   - Levo os calções e a T-shirt.
   - A T-shirt também é tamanho
   médio?

- Sim, por favor.
- Eu levo duas T-shirts tamanho
  pequeno. Olha, Steve, sapatos de
  treino baratos! Olha há o número 37!

They buy T-shirts, shorts and trainers.

5 *a* €53; *b* é muito caro (very
   expensive); *c* €15; *d* tamanho médio
   (medium); *e* Carlos – uma
   T-shirt e calções; Maria – duas T-shirts
   e sapatos de treino.

6 - Quanto é tudo?
   - Quarenta e dois euros
   €42.

7 três tomates grandes, cinco maçãs,
   quatro quilos de batatas, um quilo de
   bacalhau, meio quilo de cogumelos.

8 *a* vinho tinto; *b* água mineral; *c* café
   descafeinado; *d* leite com chocolate;
   e sumo natural.

9 - Quanto **custa** o livro?
   - €22,50.
   - Quanto **custam** os postais?
   - €1,25 **cada**.
   - **Tem** selos?
   - Não. O correio é **na** primeira rua
   à **direita**.
   - Quanto custa **tudo**?
   - **O** livro, **o** jornal, cinco postais e **a**
   revista: €32,30.

10 *a* Onde mora? *b* Há um banco aqui
   perto? *c* Onde é o Centro de
   Turismo? *d* É longe? *e* Onde trabalha?

11 *a* C; *b* A; *c* B.

Unit 8 **Queria um quarto**

Page 72 **Checking in at a hotel**

2 *first guest*
   - Bom dia.
   - Sou o Pedro Lopes. Reservei um

quarto com duas camas.

- Ah, sim. Um quarto com duas camas e com duche. É o quarto número vinte e três no segundo piso.

second guest

- Boa noite. Reservei um quarto de casal.
- O seu nome?
- Ana Fortes.
- Sim, é o quarto número três no rés-do-chão. Um quarto de casal com banho.

third guest

- Bom dia.
- Bom dia. Diga.
- Reservei um quarto de casal com duche.
- O seu nome?
- Amilcar Abreu.
- É no primeiro piso. É o quarto número quinze. Faz favor, a chave.
- Obrigado.
- O seu passaporte?
- Faz favor. Tem elevador?
- Sim, ali ao fundo.

Sr Lopes – twin-bedded, shower, room 23, second floor; Sra Fortes – double, bath, room 3, ground floor; Sr Abreu – double, shower, room 15, first floor.

3 • Ali ao fundo – over there at the end.

Page 73 **Finding a hotel room**

2 • Faz favor.
   • Tem dois quartos para esta noite?
   • Simples ou de casal?
   • Simples.
   • Sim, no terceiro piso. O quarto número trinta e quatro e o trinta e seis. Só para uma noite?
   • Sim, só esta noite.

Two single rooms; one night; rooms 34 and 36.

3 • K, W, Y are not in the alphabet.

4 • A Senhora como se chama?
   • Maria Gonzalez.
   • Como se escreve Gonzalez?

- **GONZALEZ**.
- E o Senhor?
- Pedro Martim. **MARTIM**.

5 • O hotel como se chama?
   • Hotel Vilamoura.
   • Como se escreve Vilamoura?
   • **VILAMOURA**. E há a Pousada Dom Vasco.
   • Como se escreve Dom Vasco?
   • Dom é **DOM**. Vasco é **VASCO**.

6 Tem um quarto de casal com duche? Tem um quarto simples com banho?

Page 74 **Booking ahead by phone**

2 a *first caller*
   • Estou.
   • Hotel Central, boa noite.
   • Queria um quarto para duas noites.
   • Para quando?
   • Para um de Fevereiro.
   • Um momento, por favor

   b *second caller*
   • Hotel Central. Boa noite.
   • Queria um quarto para duas semanas.
   • Para quando?
   • Dia um de Julho?
   • Um de Julho está bem. Para uma pessoa?
   • Sim.

   c *third caller*
   • Estou.
   • Hotel Central, bom dia.
   • Queria um quarto com duas camas para Agosto, dia cinco.
   • Dia cinco de Agosto . . . um momento. Para quantas noites?
   • Sete noites.

   a 1 February; b 1–13 July; c 5 August

Page 75 **Making requests**

2 *first guest*
   • Desculpe, podemos telefonar daqui?
   • Não, peço desculpa. O telefone não trabalha.

second guest

- Posso nadar na piscina?

● Sim. A piscina está aberta.

third guest

● Posso comprar selos aqui?

● Sim aqui na loja ao lado.

fourth guest

● Podemos estacionar aqui?

● Sim.

Não; Sim; Sim; Sim.

3 ● Onde podemos estacionar?

● O parque de estacionamento é ali à direita.

In the car park, over there on the right.

Page 76 **Put it all together**

I *a* Do you have? *b* I've booked;
   c I'd like; *d* Can I?

2 Lisboa, 13 de Agosto de 2003
   Sr Gerente,
   Queria reservar *(a)* **um quarto de casal** *(b)* **com banho** *(c)* **para três noites**, de *(d)* **vinte e três** a *(e)* **vinte e cinco de Setembro** *(f)* em nome de . . . .

3 *a* Não; *b* Sim; *c* Não; *d* Sim.

Page 77 **Now you're talking!**

I ● Bom dia. Faz favor.

● **Tem um quarto?**

● Para uma pessoa?

● **Sim, para três noites.**

● Sim, há um quarto no terceiro piso.

● **Quanto é?**

● €50 por noite. O seu nome?

● **Chamo-me Lionel Brett.**

● Como se escreve Brett?

● **BRETT**.

2 ● **Estou.**

● Hotel Central. Boa tarde.

● **Boa tarde. Tem um quarto para uma semana?**

● Simples ou de casal?

● **De casal.**

● O seu nome?

● **Chamo-me Maria Bustamante.**

● Como se escreve Bustamante?

● **BUSTAMANTE.**

3 ● Faz favor.

● **Reservei um quarto simples para duas noites.**

● O seu nome?

● *Say your name and spell it.*

● Com duche ou com banho?

● **Com banho. Posso estacionar perto do hotel?**

● Sim, ali ao fundo há um parque de estacionamento.

Page 78 **Quiz**

I Estou; *2* para o dia vinte e um de Abril;
3 a key; *4* No parking; *5* Julho; *6* posso
(I can), podemos (we can); *7* ground floor;
8 twin–bedded room; *9* três de Maio.

Unit 9 **A que horas parte?**

Pages 80 & 81 **Asking if there is a bus or coach and checking train times**

2 ● Há uma camioneta para Vilamoura?

● Há, sim. Para Vilamoura parte às dez horas.

● Há uma camioneta para Lagos?

● Há, sim. Às treze horas.

● Há uma camioneta para Braga?

● Há, sim. A camioneta para Braga parte às quinze horas.

● Há um autocarro para o aeroporto?

● Sim, às doze horas.

Vilamoura – leaves at 10.00; Braga – leaves at 15.00; Lagos – leaves at 13.00; airport – leaves at 12.00.

3 ● **Há uma camioneta para Viana do Castelo?**

● Há uma às nove horas.

● **A camioneta para Faro quando parte?**

● Às duas horas da tarde.

4 Há uma camioneta para o Porto?
   Há um autocarro para a estação?

6 ● A que horas parte o próximo comboio para Faro?

- Para Faro? Às sete e quarenta e cinco.
- A que horas chega a Faro?
- Às dez e quinze.
- A que horas chega o comboio de Lagos?
- Às nove e trinta.
- Há um comboio para Viseu?
- Sim, o próximo comboio é às sete e trinta e cinco.
- A que horas chega a Viseu?
- Às nove e quarenta.
- A que horas chega o próximo comboio de Braga?
- Às dez horas.

Faro: leaves at 7.45 and arrives at 10.15; Lagos: arrives at 9.30; Viseu: leaves at 7.35 and arrives at 9.40; Braga: arrives at 10.00.

7 A que horas parte o próximo comboio para Faro? A que horas chega a Faro? A que horas chega o comboio de Lisboa?

Pages 82 & 83 **Buying tickets and checking travel details**

2 *Faro*
   - Queria um bilhete de primeira classe para Faro, por favor.
   - De ida e volta?
   - Não, só de ida. De que linha parte o comboio?
   - Da linha dois.

   Braga
   - Diga, por favor.
   - Um bilhete de ida e volta para Braga.
   - De primeira classe?
   - Não, de segunda classe.
   - Faz favor.
   - De que linha parte?
   - Da linha um.

   Coimbra
   - Queria um bilhete de ida e volta para Coimbra.
   - Um bilhete de ida e volta, faz favor.
   - A que horas parte?
   - Às dez e trinta.
   - A que horas chega?

- Às onze e quarenta e cinco.

Lagos
- Faz favor, diga.
- Um bilhete de ida e volta para Lagos para o intercidades.
- Ida e volta para o intercidades.

Oporto
- A Senhora, faz favor.
- Queria um bilhete de segunda classe para o Porto.
- Para o intercidades?
- Sim, por favor. Só de ida.
- O comboio parte da linha cinco.
- Obrigada.

Faro – single; Braga – second class, return; Coimbra – return; Lagos – return, intercity; Oporto – second class, single, intercity.

3 *a* Braga – platform 1, Oporto – 5, Faro – 2; *b* at 10.30; *c* at 11.45.

4 Um bilhete de ida e volta para Lagos; Um bilhete de primeira classe para Coimbra, só de ida; Um bilhete de ida e volta para o intercidades para o Porto.

6 - Há comboio para Braga amanhã, feriado?
   - Há sim.
   - É directo?
   - Não é não. A senhora **tem de** mudar no Porto.
   - **Tenho de** reservar lugar?
   - Sim e **tem de** reservar hoje.

7 *first traveller*
   - Há um comboio para Viana do Castelo?
   - Há sim, mas o Senhor tem de mudar no Porto.
   - Tenho de reservar lugar?
   - Não.
   - De que linha parte o comboio?
   - O comboio parte da linha quatro.

   second traveller
   - Há uma camioneta para Vilamoura?
   - Sim, há uma às onze e quinze.
   - A que horas parte?
   - Às onze e quinze.
   - Desculpe, não compreendo.

- Às onze e quinze.
- Um bilhete só de ida, por favor.

a verdadeiro; b verdadeiro; c verdadeiro; d falso; e verdadeiro; f falso; g falso.

Page 84 **Put it all together**

1   *a* volta; *b* tenho de; *c* para; *d* parte; às nove; *e* há; *f* horas; chega

2   *a* à uma hora; *b* às sete e vinte e cinco; *c* às dez horas; *d* às treze horas; *e* às dezaseis e quinze; *f* às vinte e duas e trinta.

3   *1 – e; 2 – b; 3 – f; 4 – a; 5 – c; 6 – d.*

Page 85 **Now you're talking!**

1   ● **Um bilhete para Braga, por favor.**
   ● Só de ida ou de ida e volta?
   ● **Só de ida. Quanto é?**
   ● De primeira ou segunda classe?
   ● **De primeira classe.**
   ● Primeira classe para Braga . . . Dex euros e cinquenta.
   ● **A que horas parte?**
   ● O comboio parte às três horas.
   ● **De que linha?**
   ● Da linha dois.

2   ● Diga.
   ● **Há uma camioneta para Viana do Castelo?**
   ● Sim, há uma de meia em meia hora.
   ● **Tenho de reservar lugar?**
   ● Não, não tem de reservar lugar.
   ● **Quanto custa?**
   ● € 9.
   ● **A que horas chega a Viana do Castelo?**
   ● Chega a Viana do Castelo às onze e quarenta e cinco.
   ● **Um bilhete de ida e volta, por favor.**

3   ● **Há um comboio directo para**
   ● **Coimbra?**

● Não, não há.
● **Onde tenho de mudar?**
● Tem de mudar no Porto.
● **Quanto custa um bilhete de ida e volta?**
● € 17,80.
● **Queria um bilhete.**

Page 86 **Quiz**

1 bilhete; *2* if there is a bus to the station; *3* arrivals; *4* Um bilhete para Lisboa; *5* Parte às cinco e trinta; *6* I don't understand; *7* tenho de; *8* tomorrow; *9* at 22.49.

Page 90 **Asking about items on the menu**

2   ● Uma mesa para três pessoas.
   ● Com certeza. Faz favor, a ementa.
   ● Que recomenda?
   ● **Os carapaus com molho à Espanhola, o bacalhau à Zé do Pipo e a carne de porco à Alentejana ou as febras grelhadas.**
   ● O que é **a sopa** do dia?
   ● Sopa de cenoura. Também há o prato do dia.

3   ● **O que é o prato do dia?**
   ● **Espetada de lulas.**

4   ● Como é o bacalhau à Zé do Pipo?
   ● É bacalhau no forno com puré de batata e maionese e servido com salada mista.
   Baked cod with mashed potatoes and mayonnaise, and served with a mixed salad.

5   ● **Como é a carne de porco à Alentejana?**
   ● É carne de porco com ameijoas, cebola e tomates.
   Missing ingredient – cebola (onion)

Page 91 **Ordering a meal**

2 • Estão prontos a pedir?
  • Para mim os camarões.
  • Um caldo verde.
  • Melão com presunto.
  *Carlos – shrimps, Maria – cabbage soup,
  Steve – melon with smoked ham.*

3 • O Senhor, o que **vai** comer?
  • Vou comer o prato **do dia**.
  • Para **mim** as febras grelhadas.
  • **Que** recomenda?

4 • Para beber?
  • Uma garrafa de cerveja Super Bock.
  • Um sumo de laranja natural.
  • Um copo de vinho branco e uma
    garrafa de água com gás.
  *A bottle of Super Bock beer, a fruit juice,
  a glass of white wine and a bottle of
  sparkling mineral water.*

5 Eu vou comer a sopa do dia, a salada
  mista, as sardinhas grelhadas

Page 92 **Saying what you like and don't like**

2 • O que tem de sobremesa?
  • **Há arroz doce, pudim flan, Baba
    de Camelo, fruta da época,
    gelados e bolo de mel.**

3 • **Eu não gosto de pudim flan.** E tu
    Maria?
  • Eu, Carlo, eu gosto. E tu Steve?
  • **Eu gosto de arroz doce.**
  • E gostas de Baba de Camelo?
  • Sim, gosto.
  • Eu também gosto. E tu?
  • Eu gosto muito.
  Yes, they all like it.

4 Gosto de arroz doce; não gosto de
  arroz doce.

Page 93 **Paying compliments**

2 • A sopa é **boa**!
  • O peixe é **muito bom**!

• As febras de porco **são óptimas**!
• Os carapaus **são muito bons**!

3 • Está tudo bem?
  • A Baba de Camelo é muito doce!
  • O pudim é delicioso!
  • O arroz doce é muito bom.

4 A sopa é muito boa.

Page 94 **Put it all together**

1 *a* A carne é óptima; *b* As sardinhas são
  muito boas; *c* O bolo é delicioso; *d* Os
  bifes são bons.

2 **Entradas e sopas**: caldo verde, melão
  com presunto, paté de pato;
  Peixes e carnes: frango no churrasco,
  bacalhau cozido, lulas fritas.

3 *a* Sim, gosto; *b* A carne de porco,
  por favor; *c* Sim, está; *d* Hoje o bife
  é bom.
4 *c – b – f – d – e – a.*

Page 95 **Now you're talking!**

1 • Uma mesa para uma pessoa?
  • **Sim.**
  • Está pronto a pedir?
  • **Queria os camarões, depois o
    frango no churrasco com uma
    salada de tomate.**
  • Para beber?
  • **Uma garrafa de vinho da casa.**
  • Branco ou tinto?
  • **Tinto.**

2 • Está tudo bem?
  • **Sim, o vinho é óptimo e o frango
    é delicioso.**
  • Deseja sobremesa?
  • **Vou comer o pudim flan.**
  • Café?
  • **Não.**

3 • Estão prontos a pedir?
  • **Que recomenda?**

- A carne de porco à Alentejana é
  muito boa.
- **A carne de porco à Alentejana e
  um bife da casa.**
- E para beber?
- **Duas cervejas.**

Page 96 Quiz

1 What do you recommend? *2* Gosto;
3 half a portion of seafood with rice;
4 Vou comer o bacalhau; *5* puré de batata;
6 Os camarões são bons; *7* food;
8 Não gosto de carne.

Ponto de controle 3 (Pages 97–100)

1 *c* Reservei um quarto simples com
  duche para duas noites.

2 • O seu nome? . . . Ah, sim. Um quarto
  simples com duche para duas noites.
  O seu passaporte, por favor. . .
  Obrigada. É o quarto número trinta
  e três no terceiro piso.
  *a your name; b your passport number;
  c room 33 on the third floor.*

3 *a* Posso telefonar? *b* Há uma tabacaria
  aqui perto? *c* O Centro de Turismo
  está aberto aos domingos? *d* Há uma
  camioneta para Évora?

4 *1b; 2a; 3d; 4c.*

5 • O número é o dois, quatro, seis, sete,
  sete, nove, um.
  The number is 246 7791.

6 • Em Évora há **o Museu de Arte
  Moderna e o Templo de Diana.
  A parte velha da cidade** também é
  muito bonita.

7 a Quando parte a próxima camioneta
  para Évora?
  b Quanto custa um bilhete de ida e
  volta?
  • A próxima camioneta para Évora
  parte às onze e vinte. Chega às treze

e trinta e cinco. É directa. Não tem
de mudar. O bilhete de ida e volta
custa dezassete euros e doze.
*c It leaves at 11.20 and arrives at 13.05.
Return ticket costs € 17,12..*

8 • **Há um restaurante aqui perto?**
- Há sim. Há um na Praça do
  Comércio. É ao fundo à direita.
  *There's one in Praça do Comércio, at the
  end on the right.*

9 *a* Queria a sopa, depois as sardinhas
  grelhadas e uma salada mista.
  b Meia garrafa de vinho branco e água
  mineral.
  c Vou comer o bolo de chocolate.

10 *a* Uma cerveja e um copo de
  vinho tinto.
  b Quanto é?
    € 1,45.
  c Donde é ela?
  d O que faz?
  e Quantos anos tem?

suggested answers
- **Moro em Brighton.**
- **Sou inglês/inglesa.**
- **Sou advogado/a.**
- **Sim, sou casado/a.**
- **Sim, tenho un filho.**
- **Não, não tenho irmãos.**
- **Sim, faz favor.**
- **Sim, gosto.**

11 • Segunda-feira vou a Lisboa. Vou falar
  com o gerente do Banco de Portugal.
  Terça, quarta e quinta-feira vou a
  Londres, sexta-feira e sábado vou ao
  Porto, a um mercado de vinhos.
  *Mon: Lisbon; Tues–Thurs: London; Fri–Sat:
  Oporto.*

12 *a* 5 minute walk; *b* garden, swimming
  pool and restaurant; *c* no; *d* per
  room; *e* yes; *f* a state-owned pousada.

Grammar

Grammar is simply the term used to describe the patterns of a language. Knowing these patterns will enable you to move away from total reliance on set phrases.

1 **Nouns** (words for people, things, places, concepts) are either masculine (m.) or feminine (f.) in Portuguese.

Singular nouns (one only)	To form the plural (more than one)	
a ending in **-o, -u**: (nearly all m.)	Add **-s**:	vinho**s** museu**s**
b ending in **-a, -dade**: (mostly f.)	Add **-s**:	cerveja**s** cidade**s**
c ending in **-e** (some m., some f.)	Add **-s**:	chave**s**

d ending in consonants
   -r, -s:
   -l:
   -m:
(some m., some f.)
	Add **-es**:
	Becomes **-is**:
	Becomes **-ns**
		doctor**es**
		jorna**is**
		jardi**ns**

Note: these are general rules and there are some exceptions to be learned as you come across them.

2 **Adjectives** (words which describe) have to 'agree' with what they describe.

Adjectives ending in **-o** have four forms:		
m.	vinho italian**o**	vinhos italian**os**
f.	cerveja italian**a**	cervejas italian**as**

Adjectives ending in **-ês** have four forms:		
m.	vinho franc**ês**	vinhos frances**es**
f.	cerveja frances**a**	cervejas frances**as**

Adjectives ending in **-e** have only two forms:		
m.	vinho doc**e**	bebida doc**e**
f.	vinhos doc**es**	bebidas doc**es**

3 **Articles** (the, a/an) have masculine and feminine forms.

	a/an	**the** (sing.)	**the** (plural)
m.	**um** sumo	**o** sumo	**os** sumos
f.	**uma** cerveja	**a** cerveja	**as** cervejas

4 Words for 'the' (**o**, **a**, **os**, **as**) combine with **a** (to), **de** (of, from); **em** (in, on) as follows:

		singular	**plural**
a	m.	a + o = **ao**	a + os = **aos**
	f.	a + a = **à**	a + as = **às**
de	m.	de + o = **do**	de + os = **dos**
	f.	de + a = **da**	de + as = **das**
em	m.	em + o = **no**	em + os = **nos**
	f.	em + a = **na**	em + as = **nas**

5 **Verbs** (words for doing or being) are easy to recognise in English because you can put 'to' in front of them: to live, to be, to speak, to pay, to have.

In Portuguese, the infinitive (the form you find in the dictionary) ends in **-ar**, **-er** or **-ir**, with each group following a pattern.

a Regular verbs have the following patterns:

		mor**ar** *to live*	compreend**er** *to understand*	part**ir** *to leave*
I	eu	mor**o**	compreend**o**	part**o**
you	tu	mor**as**	compreend**es**	part**es**
you	você	mor**a**	compreend**e**	part**e**
he/she	ele/ela	mor**a**	compreend**e**	part**e**
we	nós	mor**amos**	compreend**emos**	part**imos**
you	vocês	mor**am**	compreend**em**	part**em**
they	eles/elas	mor**am**	compreend**em**	part**em**

b Since the ending of the verb is enough to tell us who is doing something, 'I', 'you', 's/he', 'we', 'they' are used in Portuguese mainly for emphasis, contrast or for clarification of the you/he/she form.

There are three words for 'you':

o Senhor/a Senhora*	someone you don't know well, an older person, your employer
você*	someone of similar age or background, another student, a work colleague
tu	a close friend or relative, a young person

* When talking to more than one person, these words become **os Senhores/as Senhoras** and **vocês**.

c To say something negative, **não** goes before the verb:

Não fala português?   O Carlos **não** trabalha aqui.

d Some common verbs don't follow the regular patterns:

		ser	**estar**	**ter**	**poder**
		to be	*to be*	*to have*	*to be able to*
I	eu	sou	estou	tenho	posso
you	tu	és	estás	tens	podes
you	você	é	está	tem	pode
he/she	ele/ela	é	está	tem	pode
we	nós	somos	estamos	temos	podemos
you	vocês	são	estão	têm	podem
they	eles/elas	são	estão	têm	podem

e   There are two verbs for 'to be' in Portuguese: **ser** and **estar**. Each has specific functions, some of which we have met in this book.

Ser describes essential characteristics and qualities:

Sou português	**Sou de Lisboa**
Ela é dentista	**O vinho é bom**

and is also used for location and position:

Onde é o banco?	**O parque é ali à direita**

Estar is used for temporary states, e.g. health:

Como está?	**Estou bem**

Portuguese–English glossary

This glossary contains only those words and phrases, and their meanings, as they occur in this book. Parts of verbs are also given in the form in which they occur, usually followed by the infinitive in brackets.

A

a, as (f.) *the*
aberto *open*
Abril *April*
os acompanhamentos *side orders*
o açúcar *sugar*
adeus *goodbye*
o advogado *lawyer*
o aeroporto *airport*
a África *Africa*
africano *African*
Agosto *August*
a água *water*
a Alemanha *Germany*
alemão *German*
ali *there, over there*
o almoço *lunch*
a altura *height*
amanhã *tomorrow*
as ameijoas *clams*
americano *American*
o ananás *pineapple*
o ano *year*
ao, à, aos, às *to the; on the*
o apetite: Bom apetite! *Enjoy your meal!*
aqui *here*
os arredores *suburbs*
o arroz *rice*
arroz doce *rice pudding*
o/a artista (m./f.) *artist*
a aspirina *aspirin*
assado *roasted*
a assinatura *signature*
o autocarro *bus*
a avenida *avenue*
o avião *aeroplane*
o azeite *(olive) oil*

B

Baba de Camelo *mousse made with condensed milk*
o bacalhau *cod*
o balcão *counter*
a banana *banana*
a banca *stall (in market)*
banca da fruta e verdura *fruit and vegetable stall*
o banco *bank*
o banho *bath*
o bar *bar*
a batata *potato*
batatas fritas *chips*
o batido *milk shake*
a baunilha *vanilla*
beber *to drink*
as bebidas *drinks*
bem *fine, all right*
a biblioteca *library*
a bica *small black coffee*
o bife *steak*
o bilhete *ticket*
boa noite *goodnight*
boa tarde *good afternoon; good evening*
o bolo *cake*
bom/boa *good*
bom dia *good morning*
o borrego *lamb*
branco *white*
brasa: na brasa *barbecued*
o Brasil *Brazil*
brasileiro *Brazilian*

C

o cabrito *kid*
cada *each*
o café *café; coffee*

a caixa *cash desk*
os calções *shorts*
o caldo verde *cabbage soup*
a cama *bed*
os camarões *shrimps*
a camioneta *coach*
o campo *country(side)*
o campo de ténis *tennis court*
o Canadá *Canada*
canadiano *Canadian*
o/a cantor/a *singer*
o carapau *jack-fish (fish like a mackerel)*
o carioca *mild black coffee*
a carne *meat*
caro *expensive*
o cartão de crédito *credit card*
o cartão telefónico *phone card*
a casa *house*
casa de banho *toilet; bathroom*
casa de banho privativa *private bathroom*
casa de hóspedes *guest house*
casado *married*
casal: quarto de casal *double (bedded) room*
o castelo *castle*
a catedral *cathedral*
a cebola *onion*
a cenoura *carrot*
o cêntimo *cent (Portuguese currency)*
o centro *centre*
Centro de Turismo *tourist office*

certeza: com certeza
certainly
a cerveja *beer*
o chá *tea*
chama (chamar-se)
  Como se chama? *What's*
  his/her/your name?
  Chamo-me *My name is*
a charcutaria *delicatessen*
a chave *key*
chega (chegar) *he/she/it*
  arrives;
  chega *that's enough/all*
a chegada *arrival*
o chocolate *chocolate*
churrasco: no churrasco
  barbecued
a cidade *town*
o cinema *cinema*
a classe *class*
o clube *club*
a Coca-Cola *Coke*
os cogumelos *mushrooms*
o colégio *school*
com *with*
o comboio *train*
comer *to eat*
como? *how? what?*
comprar *to buy*
compreender
  to understand
  Não compreendo *I don't*
  understand
o conhaque *brandy*
o controle *control, check*
o copo *(drinking) glass*
o correio *post office*
a costeleta *chop (e.g. lamb)*
cozido *boiled*
custa (custar) *it costs;*
  Quanto custa? *How much*
  does it cost?

D

daqui *from here*
de *from*
delicioso *delicious*
demasiado *too*
depois *then*
descafeinado *decaffeinated*

Desculpe! *Excuse me!*
deseja (desejar):
  Que deseja? *What would*
  you would like?
desempregado *unemployed*
devagar *slowly*
Dezembro *December*
o dia *day*
  do dia *of the day*
directo *direct*
a direita *right;*
  à direita *on the right*
a discoteca *nightclub*
divorciado *divorced*
diz (dizer): Come se diz?
  How do you say?
do, da, dos, das *of the;*
  from the
doce *sweet*
dois, duas *two*
o domingo *Sunday*
a Dona *Mrs, Miss*
Donde . . . ? *Where . . .*
  from?
a dose *portion*
o duche *shower*
duplo *double*

E

é (ser) *he/she/it is; you are*
  Quanto é? *How much is (it)?*
e *and*
Edimburgo *Edinburgh*
ela *she;* elas *they*
ele *he;* eles *they*
o eléctrico *tram*
o elevador *lift*
em *in*
a ementa *menu*
a empregada *sales assistant*
o engenheiro *engineer*
as entradas *starters*
entre *between*
a época *season*
  da época *in season*
escocês *Scottish*
a Escócia *Scotland*
a escola *school;*
  escola de línguas
  language school

escreve (escrever):
  Como se escreve?
  How do you spell it?
o/a escritor/a *writer*
o escritório *office*
a Espanha *Spain*
  à Espanhola *Spanish style*
  espanhol *Spanish*
a especialidade *speciality*
a espetada *kebab*
os espinafres *spinach*
a esposa *wife*
o esposo *husband*
a esquerda *left;*
  à esquerda *on the left*
está (estar): Como está?
  How are you?
esta (f.) *this*
a estação *station*
estacionar *to park*
os Estados Unidos
  (da América) *United*
  States (of America)
a estalagem *inn*
estamos (estar) *we are*
estar *to be*
este (m.) *this*
estou (estar) *I am;*
  Hello (on phone)
o/a estudante *student*
eu *I*
o euro *euro*
  (Portuguese currency)

F

falar *to talk*
falso *false*
a família *family*
a farmácia *chemist's*
o fato de treino *track-suit*
faz (fazer) *he/she/it does;*
  you do:
  Que faz? *What (work) do*
  you do?
  faz favor *please*
as febras *fillets*
fechado *closed*
o feijão verde *haricot beans*
Fevereiro *February*
o fiambre *ham*

a filha *daughter*
o filho *son*
os filhos *children*
os folhetos *leaflets*
o forno: no forno *baked (in oven)*
a França *France*
  francês *French*
o frango *chicken*
  frente: sempre em frente *straight on*
  frito *fried*
a fruta *fruit*
  fumar *to smoke*
o fundo *end;*
  ao fundo da rua at the end of the street

G

o galão *coffee served in a glass*
  galês *Welsh*
a galinha *chicken*
as gambas *prawns*
o garoto *small white coffee*
a garrafa *bottle*
o gás: com gás *sparkling,* sem gás *still*
o gelado *ice cream*
o gelo *ice*
o/a gerente *manager*
  gosta (gostar) *he/she likes; you like*
  gostas (gostar) *you like*
  gosto (gostar) *I like*
a grama *gram*
  grande *big*
  grátis *free*
  grelhado *grilled*
o guia *guide, guide-book*

H

  há *there is, there are*
  hoje *today*
a hora *time; hour;*
  A que horas? At what time?
o hospital *hospital*
o hotel *hotel*

I

  ida: só de ida *single (ticket)* de ida e volta *return (ticket)*
a idade *age*
a ilha *island*
a imperial *draught beer*
o impulso *telephone unit*
  incluído *included*
as informações *information desk*
a Inglaterra *England*
  inglês *English*
o intercidades *intercity*
a Irlanda *Ireland*
  irlandês *Irish*
a irmã *sister*
o irmão *brother;* os irmãos *brothers (and sisters)*
a Itália *Italy*
  italiano *Italian*

J

  Janeiro *January*
o jardim *garden*
o jornal *newspaper*
o/a jornalista *journalist*
  Julho *July*
  Junho *June*

L

a laranja *orange*
a laranjada *orange drink*
o leitão *sucking-pig*
o leite *milk;*
  a meia de leite large white coffee
a limonada *lemonade*
a linha *platform*
  Lisboa *Lisbon*
o litro *litre*
o livro *book*
a loja *shop*
  Londres *London*
  longe *far*
  lugar: reservar lugar *to book a seat*
as lulas *squid*

M

a maçã *apple*
a mãe *mother*
  Maio *May*
  mais *more*
a manhã *morning;* da manhã *in the morning*
  Março *March*
o marisco *seafood*
o Martini *Martini*
  mas *but*
o/a médico/a *doctor*
  de meia em meia hora *every half hour*
  meio *half*
o mel *honey*
o melão *melon*
o mercado *market*
a mercearia *grocer's (shop)*
o mês *month*
a mesa *table*
o metro, metropolitano *underground*
o metro *metre*
  meu (m.) *my*
  mim: para mim *for me*
  minha (f.) *my*
o minuto *minute*
  misto *mixed*
  moderno *modern*
o molho *sauce*
o momento *moment*
o morango *strawberry*
  morar (em) *to live (in)*
o mosteiro *monastery*
a mousse *mousse*
  mudar *to change (trains)*
  muito *very; much*
  Muito prazer *Pleased to meet you*
o museu *museum*
  museu de arte moderna *museum of modern art*
  museu de arte popular *folk art museum*

N

a nacionalidade *nationality*
  nadar *to swim*
  não *no; not*

natural *natural*

a noite *night*

o nome *name*

nós *we*

Novembro *November*

novo *new*

o número *number;*
o número de telefone
phone number

O

o, os (m.) *the*

obrigado *thank you*

Olá *Hello*

onde *where*

óptimo *excellent*

Outubro *October*

P

a padaria *baker's*

pagar *to pay*

o pai *father*

o País de Gales *Wales*

panorâmico *panoramic*

o pão *bread*
pão de forma *loaf of
bread*

a papelaria *stationer's*

para *for*

a paragem *(bus) stop*

o parque *park*
parque de estacionamento
car park

a parte *part*

a partida *departure*
partir *to leave*

o passaporte *passport*

o paté *pâté*

o pato *duck*

o pé *foot*
a pé *on foot, walking*

o peixe *fish*

o peixe espada *swordfish*

a pensão *boarding house*
pequeno *small*
o pequeno almoço
breakfast

a pêra *pear*

perto *near*

o perú *turkey*

a pescada *hake (fish)*

o peso *weight*

o pêssego *peach*

a pessoa *person*

o/a pintor/a *painter*

a piscina *swimming pool*

o piso *floor*

a planta *map*
pode (poder) *you, he/she
can*
podemos (poder) *we can*

o ponto de controle
checkpoint
por *for*
por favor *please*

o porco *pork*

o porto *port*
Porto *Oporto*

o Portugal *Portugal*
português *Portuguese*
posso (poder) *I can*

o postal *postcard*

a pousada *hotel*
pousada de juventude
youth hostel

a praça *square*

a praia *beach*

o prato *dish*
prato do dia *dish of the
day*
prazer: Muito prazer
Pleased to meet you

o preço *price*

o presunto *smoked ham*
primeiro *first*

o/a professor/a *teacher*

a profissão *profession*
pronto *ready*
próximo *next*

o pudim flan *caramel crème*

o puré de batata *mashed
potato*

Q

quando? *when?*
quanto? *how much?*
quantos? *how many?*

a quarta-feira *Wednesday*

o quarto *bedroom*
que? *what?*

o queijo *cheese*
queria (querer) *I'd like*

o quilo *kilo*

o quilómetro *kilometre*

a quinta-feira *Thursday*

o quiosque *street kiosk*

R

o rápido *fast train*

o/a recepcionista *receptionist*
recomendar *to recommend*
reformado *retired*
repetir *repeat*

o rés-do-chão (R/C) *ground
floor*
reservar *to reserve*

o restaurante *restaurant*
restaurante chinês *Chinese
restaurant*

a revista *magazine*

a rua *road, street*

as ruínas *ruins*

S

o sábado *Saturday*

o saco de desporto *sports
bag*

o sal *salt*

o sapato *shoe*

os sapatos de treino *trainers
(shoes)*

a sardinha *sardine*

a sauna *sauna*
se chama : Como se
chama? *What's his/her
name? What's your name?*

o/a secretário/a *secretary*

a segunda-feira *Monday*
segundo *second*
sei (saber): não sei *I don't
know*

o selo *stamp*

os semáforos *traffic lights*

a semana *week*
sempre *always*
sempre em frente *straight*

ahead/on

o senhor *man, Mr, Sir*

a senhora *woman, Miss, Mrs, Madam*

a Senhora Dona *Mrs, Miss*

ser *to be*

Setembro *September*

a sexta-feira *Friday*

sim *yes*

simples *single*

a sobremesa *dessert*

solteiro *single*

somos (ser) *we are*

a sopa *soup*

sou (ser) *I am*

o sumo *juice*

o supermercado *supermarket*

T

a T-shirt *T-shirt*

a tabacaria *tobacconist's*

o talão *receipt*

o tamanho *size*

também *also, too*

a tarde *evening*

a tarte *tart*

Tchau *'bye*

Tchim! Tchim! *Cheers!*

o teatro *theatre*

telefonar *to telephone*

o telefone *telephone*

têm (ter) *you (pl.) have; they have*

tem (ter) *he/she has; you (sing.) have*

temos (ter) *we have*

tenho (ter) *I have*

ter *to have;*

ter de *to have to*

a terça-feira *Tuesday*

o terceiro *third*

a tia *aunt*

o tinto *red (wine)*

o tio *uncle*

o tipo *type*

todos os dias *every day*

o tomate *tomato*

torrado *toasted*

trabalhar *to work*

o trabalho *work, job*

a T-shirt *T-shirt*

tu *you (fam.)*

tudo *all, everything*

o turismo *tourism*

U

um/uma *one; a/an*

a União Européia *European Union*

a universidade *university*

V

a vaca *cow*

a vaga *vacancy*

os vegetais *vegetables*

velho *old*

verdadeiro *true*

a vila *village*

o vinho *wine*

vire (virar) *you (sing.) turn*

virem (virar) *you (pl.) turn*

o viúvo *widower*

você, vocês *you*

vou (ir): vou comer *I'm going to eat*

Keep on talking!

If you've enjoyed *Talk Portuguese* and are keen to progress to a higher level, then BBC Languages offers a range of books and resources to help you. *Discovering Portuguese* is the ideal next step. A complete independent study course, it provides you with a detailed introduction to the language, the people and the culture.

Also available:
Get By in Portuguese

*196pp course book;
2 x 60-minute audio cassettes*

For more information on the BBC Languages range, visit: www.bbclanguages.com
For a catalogue, call: (020) 8433 3135.

*Travel pack
for beginners*

BBC books are available from bookshops, or direct from Bookpost on (01624) 675137. Or order online at: www.bbclanguages.com